CAROLE URBAS

24 23 22 21 20 19 8 7 6 5 4 3 2 1

Published by

Jeremiahs Call Ministries
31033 Buttermilk Court
Evergreen, CO 80439
www.jeremiahscall.org

Library of Congress Cataloging-in-Publication Data

ISBN Paperback: 978-1-7340352-0-9
ISBN Ebook: 978-1-7340352-1-6
Printed in the United States of America

Lord Jesus, this work is an offering unto You, a loving gift to the people You love and desire to see awakened to holiness, humility, and love.

TABLE OF CONTENTS

INTRODUCTION

"Enter by the narrow gate; for wide is the gate and broad is the way that leads to destruction, and there are many who go in by it. Because narrow is the gate and difficult is the way which leads to life, and there are few who find it."

— MATTHEW 7:13-14

"Satan dreads nothing but prayer. His one concern is to keep the saints from praying. He fears nothing from prayerless studies, prayerless work, prayerless religion. He laughs at our toil, he mocks our wisdom, but he trembles when we pray." —Samuel Chadwick, an English Methodist minister (1860-1932)

Jeremiah was a prophet in the Old Testament Scriptures. His ministry extended from 626 to 586 BC, making him a contemporary of the prophets Zephaniah, Ezekiel, and Habakkuk. He was born just three miles northeast of Jerusalem in Anathoth. His ministry came at a critical time for the nation of Israel as the people were walking in disobedience to God, in idolatry, and in defilement. God called Jeremiah out as a youth and put His words into his mouth to speak to the people of his day: *"Behold, I have put My words in your mouth. See, I have this day set you over the nations and over the kingdoms, to root out and to pull down, to destroy and to throw down, to build and to plant"* (Jeremiah 1:9b-10).

Jeremiah's voice became a trumpet sound in the midst of chaos and darkness in the hearts of the people. Judgment was coming. The people could not willfully continue in their sin without consequences. Jeremiah was calling them to re-examine themselves and turn back to God in repentance and holiness. Although his messages warned of impending doom, he also gave a word of hope. Restoration would come to a remnant.

A trumpet cries out today too—a warning and a hope, an awakening call, a Jeremiah call to the body of Christ: Wake up! Like Jeremiah, we should be preparing the way for the Lord, but we've become dull of hearing, tired of waiting, and we have not the power nor authority we think we do. We're called to be servants who hunger and thirst after righteousness, yet we have become consumers, constantly needing to be fed. So powerful is the Church of God that the gates of hell will not prevail against it! Why isn't that happening?

Somewhere the rules were changed, and we began following a different gospel. Our ears are not trained to hear His voice. Our swords are not sharpened for battle. Our fires have not been kindled to speak boldly the Word of God, and finally, we quench the very Helper He sent us. His Spirit, the One sent to equip us, train us, gift us, convict us, and lead us has been pushed to the background. The appearance of godliness thrives in His houses of worship, and His power is continually denied. How can such wickedness be pardoned without undermining the holiness of God? Do we even understand God's holiness and how we have dishonored it?

God dwells in unapproachable light. We cannot even begin to comprehend the sheer power and divine dread of the glory of God. John, the very disciple who laid his head on His savior's chest during the Last Supper fell as though dead when he saw his resurrected Lord in the vision he had in the book of Revelation. Moses could not even look upon the face of God. Our Lord is enthroned in heaven amidst thunderings, lightnings, and myriads of angels singing praise to Him day and night. He is beyond time and space. He is the beginning and the end, the Alpha and the Omega, the Aleph Tav (the first and last letters of the Hebrew alphabet). He is the same yesterday, today, and forever, so He hasn't changed.

He is the Word. He is our Creator. He is our Sanctifier. He is Righteousness. He is Peace. He is our Healer. He is the Commander of the armies of heaven. He is God Almighty. He is Yahweh—I AM. He is Jesus Christ, Yeshua Ha Mashiach. He is our Shepherd, our Provider, our Victor, our Standard, God with us, the King of Kings, the Lord of Lords, the rider on the white horse whose name is Faithful and True! He is the holy One of Israel. He is the God who sees, and His eyes are on the good and the evil. His house is called a House of prayer for all nations.

And yet, like the ancient Israelites during the days of Jeremiah, it's as if we have forgotten this. Other lovers have come and stolen our affections, and we no longer seek after Him as though we were searching for a long-lost treasure. We have settled into idolatry and disobedience and can't see that we are poor, hungry, and naked. We no longer know what holiness looks like…in ourselves nor especially in God. My friends, we have settled for so much less than what God intended.

We live in a time when Christians flock to speakers rather than the reading of the Word of God itself. If it's not a well-known worship band or leader, the turnout is less than desired. A popular pastor of a church goes on vacation, and its proven that a third of the congregation misses the next couple of weeks because of his absence. In most churches, the prayer ministry has become the smallest ministry while programming consumes a large piece of the budget. People are less and less challenged by sound doctrine as many flock to places where they receive a weekly dose of three-point sermons to find the help they need to get then through life issues. Studies show that people lose interest after fifteen minutes, so worship in many churches rarely exceeds the fifteen-minute mark. We expect the Holy Spirit to show up at nine, leave by ten, but then be with us to guide us throughout our week. We are adopting a model of counterfeit holiness. While true doctrine is being watered down and the Holy Spirit is noticeably absent, hell is filling up.

Peter calls Jesus a *"stone of stumbling and a rock of offense"* (1 Peter 2:8), but we are offering an un-offensive Jesus. More and more we're creating safe spaces, or seeker-friendly environments, where people can listen to the Word of God and not be offended. That's unbiblical. Biblically, when an unbelieving person encounters the living Christ through the power of the Word of God, the Holy Spirit goes to work immediately. Charles Spurgeon, a mid-18th century preacher, was fifteen years old when God got a hold of him. He couldn't sleep for weeks and weeks under the conviction of the Holy Spirit; nor could he eat.

People aren't born again just because they raise their hand in a church service or have a sacrament performed on them. The Bible says they are in darkness (Romans 2:19). They have 10 million sins and transgressions of the law marring their nature. They must come to see the sorrow of what sin has caused in their life, and only "godly sorrow produces repentance leading to salvation" (2 Corinthians 7:10). Once they recognize their need for a Savior, which I believe still happens in churches among other places, then they need a radical change of life through the power and conviction of the Holy Spirit pressed upon them. I have seen too many people over the years raise a hand in church, go through baptism, and then go back to their old way of life, turning their backs on God. Once we've tasted that the Lord is good, we should never want to go back to our old life. To prevent this, we must understand holiness and daily study the Word of God. Otherwise, as in the parable of the sower (Matthew 13), when tribulation and difficult times come, we will have no roots to hold us up, and the seed once sown in our hearts will die.

Hebrews 4:12 tells us *"the word of God is living and powerful, and sharper than any two-edged sword, piercing even to the division of soul and spirit, and joints and marrow, and is a discerner of the thoughts and intents of the heart."* When it is spoken in the power and authority of the Holy Spirit, it convicts, bringing repentance. Conviction, my friends, is a gift from God for it is the "goodness of God" that leads us to repentance (Romans 2:4)! Thus, church on Sunday isn't necessarily supposed to be a "safe space" but a place where His sword is drawn to separate lies from the truth and the wheat from the chaff. Church is also His body of believers. It's His people speaking forth truth in love under the anointing of the Holy Spirit. When that truth is spoken, it brings conviction, not judgment or condemnation, and leads them to a new life in Christ.

When was the last time you went to church and the pastor, priest, or preacher stopped under the conviction of the Holy Spirit, threw aside his notes, and spoke under that power? Have you ever witnessed that? If so, you know that when the Holy Spirit is given His rightful place, repentance comes. People will not leave there until they know what to do next! There is a cry of the heart, a. rending of the heart. They realize their spirit is impoverished and in desperate need of a Savior. One can barely raise their head as they ask for forgiveness because they are so overcome with the shame of their sin. Then the Holy Spirit moves in and becomes the lifter of their heads (Psalm 3:3).

For several years, a group of us have been unapologetically teaching the difficult yet transformational power of God's Word. We have watched people literally jump up to ask, "What do I do next?" like in the days of John the Baptist. The Church must get herself ready. Jesus is coming. Did you hear that? He's coming! His return is rarely taught on and I fear that when He does return for His bride one day, not only will we not recognize the trumpet sound of His voice, but we will not be ready. If He wanted His disciples to be ready some 2,000 years ago as if He were coming in their lifetime, you can be sure He wants that even more for you today.

It's time for the body of Christ to be the force upon the earth it was always destined to be. It's time to be salt, light, and a city on a hill that cannot be hid. There is coming a time when God will not always *"strive with man"* (Genesis 6:3). May we be voices, trumpeters on the walls of our nation, cities, communities, homes, and all we hold dear.

This study you are about to embark on is a cry for holiness. You are going to go to the deep places of your heart with your Creator and Savior to dig out your well and find out what pleases Him. What does it look like to serve a holy God and turn away from idolatry? What does it look like to wash the feet of Jesus? What does it look like to be poor in spirit or to mourn? How does meekness lead to hungering and thirsting for righteousness? Do you have a spiritual appetite, a craving to bow down in worship and sit at Jesus feet?

Mercy and compassion bring forth purity and peace. His nature must emerge in us. It must. We are nothing and can do nothing apart from Him. The gospel is good news. It is the joy of our salvation, but we're called to share in the sufferings of Christ also. Are you prepared to be persecuted for your faith? When your spouse or your friends or other Christians don't understand you anymore and pull away or act confused, will you be able to rejoice in that tribulation?

In this journey, if you allow His Spirit to convict you and His anointing to minister to your heart, you will not be the same person! This study is designed to cause you to wrestle. For over twenty years, I have sat in one Bible study after another, sometimes three at a time. They have been key in my insatiable appetite for truth. But this study is different. Your ears will learn how to hear. Your sword will get sharpened. His Word will be ever on your tongue and, if you allow Him to emerge, He will use you *"to root out and to pull down, to destroy and to throw down, to build and to plant."*

Beloved, get ready to be ignited!

How to Use This Study

WALKING THROUGH *The Narrow Gate* and choosing to walk the narrow path God has planned for you is a courageous decision. It is not easy to follow Christ, let alone become Christ-like. There is much involved in carrying the mantle of being a believer. This study is not designed to be merely another checkmark on a list of things to accomplish in your Christian walk. *This study is an invitation to holiness.*

This Bible study is works in conjunction with a series of ten video teachings. Each video coincides with a week of the book. The video teachings are designed to complement and enhance each chapter by taking the information written in the study to a deeper level. You will also notice that each chapter in the book is laid out differently than most studies. Having completed countless Bible studies, I understand firsthand the desire to want to read a chapter in its entirety, highlight the inspiring parts, and then discuss in a group "what spoke to us." You can approach this book in that way, but I encourage you not to. In this study, each chapter contains break-points called "Reflect and Respond" where you are asked to stop and meditate on what you have just read. These may include questions to answer, Scriptures to read, or points to ponder. Though this study is designed for either group or individual study, it is foremost a very *personal* journey. God wants to speak to *you*!

As you walk through it, you will be regularly evaluating your walk along the narrow path. This will require a sacrifice of your time. Meditating and reflecting on our personal relationship with Jesus Christ is not the type of homework you can accomplish the day your Bible study is to meet. Because it requires self-examination, you will need to set aside quiet time during the week to allow for this type of examination to occur, perhaps one to two hours per day. Please understand this is not a study you can rush through.

As believers, we have mastered how to look the part of a Christian from the outside, but God is mostly concerned with our inner man. Therefore, our focus will be on the commitment and surrender it will require of you to be transformed into the image of Christ. In addition to evaluating yourself, you will be given some "Practical Practices" to help you put into practice the truths taught in each chapter. Each one will challenge you to take the time to grow your relationship with Christ. There are no fill-in-the-blanks or mandatory assignments to be completed. This is a journey into your heart, your faith, your relationship with Jesus Christ. You will only get out of it what you put into it.

Paul tells us that we are *"always learning and never able to come to the knowledge of the truth"* (2 Timothy 3:7). That is what we want to change. We want to learn but also come to the truth about God's holiness—what it means for us to be holy—and what a relationship with Christ is to truly look like. The answers have always been in front of us, in the Scriptures, but we need the revelation of the Holy Spirit to show us how God wants us to explore and exercise these truths. It is time to grow; *"When I was a child, I spoke as a child, I understood as a child, I thought as a child; but when I became a man, I put away childish things"* (1 Corinthians 13:11).

So, come Holy Spirit into this study and breath upon us Your revelation of the knowledge of Christ in us. Open the eyes of our understanding so that Your Word brings light into our being. Remove from us any preconceived ideas, generational habits and practices, expectations and prior judgments as to what a walk with You is to look like. Rather, pour out a fresh anointing of Your Spirit upon us, so we can come to the knowledge of truth. In the NAME of the most High God, Jesus Christ, we pray. Amen.

Let's Begin

Use a journal or a notepad for the following. Before beginning this study, try to answer the two questions below. Do not use a Bible, computer, book, or any other resource. Write your answers from your own experience with God and your relationship with Jesus Christ.

(1) What does it look like for God to be holy? What does it look like for you to be holy? Do not describe what you think the right answer is. Write as much as you know about His holiness, even if it's very little. Then describe what holiness looks like for you as a believer.

(2) Describe your relationship with your Father (or God, if that sounds more comfortable to you at this present time) and Jesus Christ. Do not describe all the things you "do" or areas in which you lead or serve or what you have learned in church or elsewhere. Just describe what you experience being in a relationship with Him.

When you are completed with that, try to answer the following questions about your relationship with Christ. It may help to use a current relationship you are in to help you think through this. Whether it's a spouse, loved one, friend or family member, we are used to being in relationships of some kind. Now apply that to Christ:

How much time do you two spend together?

How often do you laugh together?

What has been your best moment together so far?

How serious are you about taking this relationship further?

Are you keeping secrets from Him?

Have you ever cheated on Him?

Have you given more of yourself to someone or something else? Describe.

What is the worst thing He knows about you?

What is the best thing He knows about you?

When was the last time you had an in-depth conversation with Him?

Do you discuss marriage?

Now, one last thing. Read the following Scriptures and write down key things that the Holy Spirit shows you about the majesty of God. Please take your time and read through these verses very slowly.

Read Exodus 19:10-25.

Read Exodus 20:1-21.

Read Isaiah 6:1-11.

Read Revelation, chapters 4-5.

Sit quietly now for as long as you are able and let the Holy Spirit begin the precious work of opening your ears. You may not hear anything at first, but He's making a deposit in you. Journal or pray what you are sensing in your spirit. Let everything you did in this exercise digest for a while before proceeding any further.

CHAPTER 1

A BAPTISM OF ANGUISH

"For My people have committed two evils: They have forsaken Me, the fountain of living waters, and hewn themselves cisterns—broken cisterns that can hold no water."

— JEREMIAH 2:13

I leaned on the back wall of the mega-church I was employed with and listened carefully to the sermon that was being delivered from the stage. I loved this place! I was on staff of one of the top churches in the United States, growing leaps and bounds in my faith and knowledge of the Scriptures, and having the privilege of rubbing elbows with some of the most popular names in Christian circles today—musicians, pastors, conference speakers, and staff members. I was blessed. As I watched this sermon, as I had countless other ones, I heard a voice speak to me. It wasn't audible of course, but I knew it was there, like a slight whisper saying, "There's more to Me than this."

The same sentence was repeated to me several times. I looked around me to make sure it wasn't someone nearby mumbling under their breath. I shrugged it off at first, and my attention was drawn back to the stage. I respected and enjoyed this pastor immensely; I still do as a matter of fact. I was always drawn into his teachings, but I couldn't shake what I had heard, and it distracted me from given him my full attention. The words kept repeating, "There's more to Me than this."

The voice continued every week after that, sometimes even during work. As a staff, we were incredibly busy! Thousands of people were coming to this church every week, and we were challenged to raise the bar on a regular basis in order to bring our "guests" the best "experience" we could. The voice continued for months. A wrestling of my faith began. I was beginning to really wonder, "Is there more to You than this?" I couldn't understand it. I was content, happy, and fulfilled in my job. Churches around the world came to ours to study how to "do church" better. Our environments screamed of professionalism and cutting edge cultural influence, which drew in the younger generation. It was a dynamic environment where hundreds of people were applying to work. There was a sense of pride and accomplishment. Isn't this how church was supposed to look? So, after a while, I assumed that the voice I heard must have been me.

It would be a couple of years later before I heard that voice again. My family and I had moved out West, and I found myself helping a young church put its systems in place and developing the ministries needed to become a mega-church. I was about a year into the task when, in the back of church listening to the sermon, I heard the voice return: "There's more to Me than this." It sounded different this time. It felt timely, urgent. But I chose to ignore it…big mistake! But what was I to do? We were busy. It was a thriving church bursting at the seams. The pastors were young, fun, and attracting a younger generation. Isn't that what God wanted? Wasn't He the One who sent me there to help? He can't pull me out now! Hundreds were getting baptized and expansion was in the works in the form of satellite campuses. Again, isn't this what church was supposed to look like? Weeks of hearing the voice again turned into months. It was not letting me off the mat this time.

One day I was at home straightening my bed when suddenly it was as if someone took my knees out from under me, and I fell straight to the floor, on my knees, head in carpet. "There's more to Me than this!" I couldn't lift my head. Up to this point, I felt like a pretty solid Christian. I was faithful with Bible study, attending church, donating my time, and praying, or so I thought. But here I was face flat on my carpet, unable to move, and I was filled with holy fear.

Have you ever been filled with holy fear? I mean a true fear of realizing how small you really are? Feeling that in a moment, the breath of God would consume you and blow you like a feather out into the abyss? That's where I was. I was fully aware of my smallness. For the first time, I felt the true holiness, majesty, and power of God upon me. He was going to get my attention one way or the other. I didn't know it then, but I was about to take a journey on the narrow path. *"Come to God through the narrow gate, because the wide gate and broad path is the way that leads to destruction—nearly everyone chooses that crowded road! The narrow gate and the difficult way leads to eternal life—so few find it"* (Matthew 7:13-14, TPT).

Reflect and Respond

- What is it you like about your church? About your pastor, priest, or preacher?
- Why do you go to church?
- What do you look for in a pastor, priest, or preacher?
- Based on your answer to the first question, how much of your answer involves being eager to meet with God? Worshipping

God? Being awestruck by His word? Being in prayer? Praying with others?

Waking Up

Oh, the deception of pride within ourselves, and within the church itself! We do so much in the name of ministry, for His Kingdom that we lose sight of the very thing He wants—our devotion. For years since that day, I have spent my time in the secret place of prayer with Almighty God Himself. I resigned from my job and didn't look back. Never had I known such a "baptism of anguish" where He allows you to feel His joy and His pain in that secret place of prayer—a place I had taken for granted and had minimized for years.

Tears and tissues have filled my floor. Paint has literally come off my windowpane from gripping it so hard as I cried out for the people of God. There were days when I would lay down on my floor unable to speak, only to wake later with a new ache in my heart even though not a word was spoken. Prayer is a place where you can't be seen by man, only God. It is the place where a humbling and a dying to self begins. In this place, He put a cry in my heart—*His* cry, a cry to wake up the body of Christ!

Looking back, I can see more clearly how His plan unfolded. He plucked me out of a profession where I served the world and its desires and placed me into a position in the heart of His church, the very people He wanted to me to "wake up" and intercede for years later. I didn't put that cry in my heart. I couldn't. I was too full of "self." Many of us are. Only the Lord can give a baptism of fire like that. It's a baptism so deep that it creates a guttural cry of the heart, one that's unrelenting with passion, boldness, and fury as never felt before. Yes, fury—fury at what I missed seeing before. Fury at what the enemy has done to our churches, our families, our youth, our nation. Fury at how the body of Christ has been lulled to sleep in this hour—myself included.

We are not prepared for what's coming. We may look good on the outside, but inside we are in dire need of a baptism of holiness. We need to heed Jeremiah's warning that judgment is coming, and Peter tells us that it begins in the house of God! *"For the time is come that judgment must begin at the house of God: and if it first begin at us, what shall the end be of them that obey not the gospel of God?"* (1 Peter 4:17, KJV).

We don't know what time it is on God's clock because we've either never been taught to watch for His return, we don't expect it in our lifetime, or we doubt it will even happen. Friends, we have much to wake up to. Don't be deceived. The longsuffering of the Lord is salvation (2 Peter 3:15). He is very patient, but in this delay, we too often ridicule those who are watching. Keep in mind Proverbs 25:2: *"It is the glory of God to conceal a matter, but the glory of kings to search out a matter." You* are a king! Did you know that? You are called a king and a priest to our God, *"To Him who loved us and washed us from our sins in His own blood, and has made us kings and priests to His God and Father, to Him be glory and dominion forever and ever. Amen"* (Revelation 1:5b-6). So, it is for your honor to seek out the Lord and what He is saying in this hour. It is for your honor to walk through the narrow gate and onto the narrow path that leads to life. Only few find it…just a few. Will you be one of them?

My passion for preaching and teaching truth was not birthed because I wanted something. It was birthed in prayer as I was confessing my own deadness and dryness. His cry became my cry. His tears flowed from my eyes, and His words were put into my mouth. I felt it. I knew it. Now I have no choice but to live it because one of the first things He calls us to is obedience. He knocks gently at first. He knocked gently when I heard His voice the first time, but He kept knocking. Out of pride, I refused to open the door, and I had been a Christian for a very long time at this point. He *will* get our attention one way or the other because every knee has to bow and every tongue has to confess that Jesus is Lord (Philippians 2:10-11). We can either bow now, willingly, or He'll take us out at the knees. *"Humble yourselves under God's mighty hand, that he may lift you up in due time. Cast all your anxiety on him because he cares for you"* (1 Peter 5:6-7, NIV).

Igniting Prayer

Oh, to examine ourselves! It is a difficult thing to look into the mirror at our true state of being. No matter how high we have soared or on which stage we have stood or which important person we know, none of us have "arrived." In fact, we never will until we are all singing "Holy, holy, holy are You, Lord," before His throne. For this reason, we should take heed to 2 Peter 1:5-11:

> For this very reason, giving all diligence, add to your faith virtue, to virtue knowledge, to knowledge self-control, to self-control perseverance, to perseverance godliness, to godliness brotherly kindness, and to brotherly kindness love. For if these things are yours and abound, you will be neither barren nor unfruitful in the knowledge of our Lord Jesus Christ. For he who lacks these things is shortsighted, even to blindness, and has forgotten that he was cleansed from his old sins. Therefore, brethren, be even more diligent to make your call and election sure, for if you do these things you will never stumble; for so an entrance will be supplied to you abundantly into the everlasting kingdom of our Lord and Savior Jesus Christ.

This brings me to prayer. With the exception of a handful of churches across our nation, it is the smallest ministry in a congregation. Usually, it's given a thirty-second plug at the end of a service. If blessed, only but a couple of people might show up. It's obvious that corporate zeal for prayer has waned over the years. Show me a praying pastor though, and I'll show you a praying church. That's a strong statement, but it's the truth. I have had the privilege of leading different prayer initiatives, even for my state, and unless there's a big-name leader or well-known musical talent, only a remnant shows up. But when a church has a praying pastor who hides away in the secret place, a congregation will get it. They know prayer is the engine that drives everything, including their church. What we need are "Spurgeon" churches with "heating plants."

> Five young college students were spending a Sunday in London, so they went to hear the famed C.H. Spurgeon preach. While waiting for the doors to open, the students were greeted by a man who asked, "Gentleman, let me show you around. Would you like to see the heating plant of the church?" They were not particularly interested, for it was a hot day in July. But they didn't want to offend the stranger, so they consented. The young men were taken down a stairway, a door was quietly opened, and their guide whispered, "This is our heating plant." Surprised, the student saw 700 people bowed in prayer, seeking a blessing on the service that was soon to begin in the auditorium above. Softly closing the door, the gentleman then introduced himself. It was none other than Charles Spurgeon. (from Grace Bible Church website)

While Spurgeon preached, his people prayed. His preaching stirred more than 10,000 listeners who gathered each Sunday to hear him in 19th-century London. God is not partial to any particular man; He's partial to prayer! When pastors devote a majority of their time to prayer and when their churches devote a majority of their time to prayer, you end up with a supernatural awakening of the body of Christ.

God is still ready to answer prayer today. He is looking to demonstrate His power in any church, anywhere, anytime who will give Him that same opportunity to honor prayer. The great revivalists knew this, and as such, they delivered sermons soaked in holy oil and preached with the fire of the Spirit. There was no such thing as a "seeker" church making people feel safe because when these men preached, people weren't seeking for long.

That is what is missing today. We have forgotten how to pray. We have forgotten what it means to be holy. We forgot that God does not do things the way the world does them. Why then is the church trying so hard to look like the world? When you set your heart to pray, God will start sharing His heart with you. He will open Himself up to you and show you the condition of the church. You will feel His ache for sleeping, discouraged, and lukewarm believers. You will feel His sadness for the imprisoned, persecuted, and brokenhearted…anyone not yet free to be all God created them to be. During prayer, He will implant His will in you to do the things that please Him on behalf of those people. You'll discover that there's pain in God's heart, and He lets you feel it.

God has much to share with us, but there are so few to hear. He's not only going to show you the condition of the church, He's going to show you the condition of your own heart and ask you a question: "What is it to you?" Will you let Him examine your heart? You are going to do one of two things. You are either going to get up and walk out of that baptismal of anguish and say "It's too much. I don't want it, God. I just want to do my regular Christian life and not carry this kind of a burden." Or, you are going to walk out of that baptismal of anguish carrying your mat with you. Like Moses at the burning bush saying, *"Lord, I am not a man of words—not yesterday, nor the day before, nor since You have spoken to Your servant—because I have a slow mouth and a heavy tongue"* (Exodus 4:10, TLV), you will feel inadequate to the task. But God uses the foolish things of the world to confound the wise. Like Paul when writing to the Corinthians, you will look like a "fool for Christ." Are you willing to do that?

I walked out of my daily baptismal of anguish knowing that I couldn't refuse to act on the cry He put in my heart. If I was going to bear His burden and become an instrument of restoration in the body of Christ, I was going to have to *"come out from among them and be separate"* (2 Corinthians 6:17). That comes at a cost for each of us. It not only costs us something like time, sleep, or changes to our schedule, but it also comes at a cost to our friends and family. We change, and they don't understand the change. For a while, we may seem to be traveling alone. Though the narrow path *is* a lonely road, you are never alone. Others are on it with you, and God will bring you to them. Out of His abundant mercy, He will reunite you with those who misunderstood you. It may look different, but you will view them out of a lens of love this time and not out of lens of needing their approval.

In that place of prayer, trust builds. He will give you little assignments to train you in obedience. In time, those assignments increase. In each step, you will begin to see how the government of the Kingdom begins to work. When you see the fruit that comes from simple assignments obeyed, your trust will grow and His trust will grow towards you. More, then, will be deposited into your care as a result.

But because many of us do not devote ourselves to prayer, we miss this incredible exchange. We miss the opportunity to deepen and strengthen our faith and allow the Lord to birth His will in us. There is a cry God wants to put into your heart, but if you do not submit yourself to a life of prayer, you may never discover what His will is for your life. He fashioned each of us in what the psalmist calls the hidden or secret place and has formed our days in His book (Psalm 139:13-16). He did not plan for you to be unfruitful.

Reflect and Respond

- Describe your prayer life.
- Do you pray (not meaning before a meal or before bed)?
- If you don't pray regularly, what is stopping you?
- If you do pray regularly, what percentage of your prayer life is asking of God and what percentage is glorifying Him?
- Describe what repentance means to you.
- When was the last time you repented to God for something?
- Where's the anguish?

This brings me back to church. My friends, we no longer see how dead the church has become because we have become comfortable in our passivity and awestruck in the experiences. We do not spend the time in prayer that we should to understand what anguishes our Lord. I have yet to hear a pastor declare from the pulpit, "Oh, Lord, your Name is being blasphemed. Your Holy Spirit is being mocked and quenched. The enemy is out trying to destroy the testimony of the Lord and deceiving doctrines have crept into the church confusing many. Let us fast and pray. Break our hearts for Your causes. Show us how we can serve You, Lord, in this hour."

What a prayer that would be! Follow that up with an hour of a praying body of believers crying out in repentance, rather than a listening to a sermon, and you have the beginnings of an ignited church. Follow that with a congregation committed to prayer and fasting for a month together, and you'll begin to have a church on fire. That is when true life in Christ begins for the body. Jesus says the world will know us when we are one. This would certainly show people we are one. You'll see more of the hand of God in that simple act of obedience and humility than a decade of your favorite pastors preaching their favorite sermons!

But that's not happening in most churches. There's no anguish, no fasting, no prayer, no brokenness. Churches and satellites are expanding, ritualistic services continue to box God in, new ministries form, and people sign up to volunteer somewhere because they want to truly do their part. However, we have only deceived ourselves and created a version of church that looks nothing like the early church of the New Testament. Oh, the time and money we could use elsewhere if we focused on becoming a praying church rather than a worldly one! Any decision made without being on our knees in prayer, fasting, and waiting on Him is a decision made in the flesh, in the mind, not from God's heart.

I've seen it and lived it firsthand. There's no condemnation in that remark, just a new understanding of where we have gone so wrong, even on the most basic level. Please hear me, there are many good things churches are *doing* for the world, but that's not what God wants. He first wants our hearts completely abandoned to Him, then out of that kind of faith, works will follow. The early church understood this. They fasted and prayed over every decision: *"They devoted themselves to the apostles' teaching and to fellowship, to the breaking of bread and to prayer"* (Acts 2:42, NIV). *"And when they had prayed, the place where they were assembled together was shaken; and they were all filled with the Holy Spirit, and they spoke the word of God with boldness"* (Acts 4:31). We need to re-evaluate anything we try to do without praying and fasting, such as determining if we're carrying a burden that God hasn't called us to. We need to ask ourselves, Is it a cry of our hearts or a cry of His?

Nehemiah was the trusted cupbearer of Artaxerxes I during the time of the Israelites' exile into Babylon. Artaxerxes allowed Nehemiah to go to Jerusalem and rebuild its walls after Nebuchadnezzar laid the city waste. Upon Nehemiah's return, he heard a devastating report:

> It came to pass in the month of Chislev, in the twentieth year, as I was in Shushan the citadel, that Hanani one of my brethren came with men from Judah; and I asked them concerning the Jews who had escaped, who had survived the captivity, and concerning Jerusalem. And they said to me, "The survivors who are left from the captivity in the province are there in great distress and reproach. The wall of Jerusalem is also broken down, and its gates are burned with fire." So it was, when I heard these words, that I sat down and wept, and mourned for many days; I was fasting and praying before the God of heaven.
>
> And I said: "I pray, Lord God of heaven, O great and awesome God, You who keep Your covenant and mercy with those who love You and observe Your commandments, please let Your ear be attentive and Your eyes open, that You may hear the prayer of Your servant which I pray before You now, day and night, for the children of Israel Your servants, and confess the sins of the children of Israel which we have sinned against You. Both my father's house and I have sinned. We have acted very corruptly against You, and have not kept the commandments, the statutes, nor the ordinances which You commanded Your servant Moses.
>
> "Remember, I pray, the word that You commanded Your servant Moses, saying, 'If you are unfaithful, I will scatter you among the nations; but if you return to Me, and keep My commandments and do them, though some of you were cast out to the farthest part of the heavens, yet I will gather them

> from there, and bring them to the place which I have chosen as a dwelling for My name.' Now these are Your servants and Your people, whom You have redeemed by Your great power, and by Your strong hand. O Lord, I pray, please let Your ear be attentive to the prayer of Your servant, and to the prayer of Your servants who desire to fear Your name; and let Your servant prosper this day, I pray, and grant him mercy in the sight of this man." For I was the king's cupbearer (Nehemiah 1:1-5).

Not one time did Nehemiah ask God why He did those things. Instead, he wept and mourned for many days. Then he fasted and prayed before God. In His prayer, He first glorified the Lord, then he confessed the sins of the people, and lastly, asked for mercy. It was no different than the prayer of Daniel in chapter nine or of the many prayers of other great men and women of the Bible. We have forgotten how to do this, how to give God the glory, confess our sins of disobedience, and then ask for His mercy. We want our prayers answered but without acknowledging our part in the situation.

Nehemiah understood this because he was in anguish, and his prayer was a cry of anguish as he stood in the gap for his people. Anything we try to do to serve the Lord without a baptism of anguish is not going to work—at least not from the perspective of the Kingdom of God. His will must be birthed in *you* first. Then we act, *"for it is God who works in you both to will and to do for His good pleasure"* (Philippians 2:13).

Many of us in the body of Christ are eager for revival, "awakenings," last days' outpourings of the Holy Spirit, signs, wonders, and miracles—but all without the humbling and anguish, without fasting and prayer. All without the cost. God's Kingdom doesn't work that way. I fear the church has been caught naked. We have been taught a different gospel. We have not the power we speak of nor the authority to come against evil that is enslaving the minds of millions. Rhetoric, we have rhetoric. We want our families saved, finances fixed, marriages restored, kids healed, the immorality to leave our nation, and we expect it to get done as a result of our one-hour services on Sunday and 15-minute prayers, rarely opening our Bibles throughout the week. Some Christians actively pursue Him, but a majority do not.

Reflect and Respond

- If a child was invited to a birthday party where the kids were asked to sit around the table with the parent and child just enjoying the child and eating cake and ice cream, would that child want to go?
- If a child was invited to a birthday party held at an elaborate event center where there would be endless amounts of fun experiences and entertainment, would that child want to go?
- Now put that in perspective of church today. If you had a choice between going to a church on Sunday where you gathered to pray, share communion, and hear someone read Scripture, sharing attributes about God your Father or of going to a church that offered all kinds of feel-good experiences with a dynamic environment and speaker, which would you attend?

Over the past six years, the American Bible Institute (ABI) has been conducting research on the impact the Bible has in our lives. They are discovering alarming trends. One such trend is that general skepticism of the Bible increased from 10% to 21% in just six years. In addition, ABI has done extensive research on people's perception of the Bible, meaning "What do people really think about the Bible?" They discovered that there are some positive perceptions; people believe the Bible is a good thing.

But there are also neutral and negative perceptions. The negative is broken down in two ways. The first negative is that the Bible is "a book." In today's culture, many don't want to take the time to sit down with a book; they want information fed to them. People also consider this book to be "old, boring, confusing, and irrelevant" to their lives. Secondly, many people say the Bible "makes them feel badly about themselves and those that they love." As a result, a new trend is forming where the Bible is being considered "anti." Fill in the blank: anti-homosexual, anti-minority, anti-women, anti-tattoos, anti-drinking, anti-fun. The result is a demise of the Bible's impact on society as a whole. Since people are not sitting down to read it for themselves, to try to understand who God is and what He is saying, they have moved away from teachers of the Word who they feel condemn them. Instead, they have moved to teachers who encourage their apathy toward the Word and spoon-feed them easy, comfortable, and safe Christianity. Do you see what is happening? These are alarming trends that need to be regularly evaluated so the Church is put on alert to distance itself from such dangerous norms.

In our present state, we are compromising and exchanging the truth for lies. That is why I say the Church is caught naked; our ignorance is exposing our true nature. I used to wonder how the Antichrist would be able to deceive the world in the last days, *"if possible, even the elect"* (Matthew 24:24). With statistics like this, it's not hard to imagine anymore.

While focusing on church growth and expansion, entertainment and programming, rituals and rites, we are losing the very thing that God says we will need most: His truth, His Word—your sword. Coffee bars, soft seats, and three-point sermons will not help you when the enemy rises up. They will not help your children. We are ill equipped at the moment for what's coming. You will need His authority, which comes from ingesting His Word. You will need the power of the Holy Spirit, which comes in a place of surrender. And, you will need to die to self, which comes in a place of prayer.

Welcome to the narrow gate.

Practical Practices

Chapter 1

Church

Write your findings in a journal or notepad.

What is the largest ministry in your church?

Seek out the prayer ministry and ask to receive prayer or a blessing.

Ask the prayer ministry team at your church the following questions: How busy are you? How often do you pray together for the congregation? How often do you pray together for the church staff and leaders?

Home

Find 15 minutes in your day this week to practice sitting with God. Sit in complete silence. Do not pray, do not worship, do not listen to music. Just practice sitting and mediating on who He is. Journal what He gives you.

Read

Record what the Holy Spirit shows you about God's way of doing things.

- Read Acts 1-3.

- Read 1 Corinthians 1:18-2:16.
- Read 1 John 2:15-27.

Listen

Each week, you will be learning how to worship the Lord through song and mediation. There are other forms of worship, but we will be focusing on music quite a bit for this study. The songs chosen for this study may be different than what you are used to, but they are songs that focus on Him. Here are your song selections for this week:

- "Storm All Around You" by Jon Thurlow, *Onething Live: Magnificent Obsession*
- "Temple" by Grace Williams, *Fire Fall*
- "Be Still and Know" by Stephen Curtis Chapman, *Speechless*

CHAPTER 2

BLESSED ARE THE POOR IN SPIRIT

"And Elijah came to all the people, and said, 'How long will you falter between two opinions? If the Lord is God, follow Him; but if Baal, follow him.' But the people answered him not a word."

— 1 KINGS 18:21

People always know when a man arrives on the scene sent from God. There are qualities about him that make him distinct from everyone else. He's a servant of the Lord, not a tool of men. He is focused and fiercely determined to deliver the message God has given Him for that hour. He speaks boldly, with authority, never watering down the truth of the Word of God. He understands the urgency of the message and the urgency of the hour, and as such, delivers his message under the anointing of the Holy Spirit, not to please men but to please God. He is sent to break up fallow ground in hearts and sow it with precious seed, the seed of the Word of God.

There is an unapologetic approach to his delivery of the gospel that few preachers have the courage to do because they have been built up by human praise and would sink under human criticism. But this man is happy after preaching a word from heaven, even if his congregation storms out. He's a threat to the status quo, the lukewarm version of Christianity we find ourselves in. People are drawn out of a slumber into a fire when he arrives, and lamp stands are ignited once again in the hearts of men and women alike.

How does a man become a vessel set on fire like that? By being a man who has become poor in spirit. He's a praying, poured-out man, one that spends time in the throne room of heaven, beholden to no one except God Almighty. Prayer becomes him. Prayer exposes him. Prayer convicts him. Prayer humbles him. Prayer revives him. Prayer prepares him. And then prayer sends him. Because he's being refined in the secret place of the Most High, he is not deterred when he is mocked, ridiculed, criticized, or ignored. He humbles himself before Almighty God. He continues because the Word of God is so deeply embedded in his heart that it has become like a burning fire shut up in his bones. He, in fact, becomes weary if he tries holding it back, and unless God's word is unleashed, this man would perish.

Where are these people today? While churches boast size and satellites, coffee and community, numbered faces and safe spaces, the fires on prayer altars have been extinguished. It appears men's bones are no longer filled with a burning, fiery ache for God's Word that cries to be released. People have become comfortable in their sin. Having their ears "tickled" by their compromised preachers, they believe that as long as they're "saved by grace," they no longer need to fear hell, nor have a fear of the Lord. The gospel has been watered down, and the church is no longer a place where the Holy Spirit is expected to convict people of sin. False prophets have moved in where the church has gone idle deceiving many with their twisted doctrine. The sheep can't discern the truth from the lie because they don't know what the truth is. Counterfeit power and counterfeit love is casting a spell upon the world, drawing in thousands of unsuspecting sheep to the slaughter.

God is looking for men and women to ignite the prayer altars once again and stand in the gap of a sleeping church. P.T. Forsyth, a Scottish theologian who died in 1921, once said, "No man has any right in the pulpit by virtue of his own personality or manhood in itself, but only in the sacramental value of his personality for his message. The church does not live by its preachers but by the Word." I'm afraid this is where we find ourselves: churches filled with personality but little to no authority, power, nor prayer. In what strange vineyards are we going to be asked to labor in God's name?

Reflect and Respond

- Without looking at any resource, describe what it means to be a lukewarm Christian.
- We meet or listen to people who are very good at expositing God's Word. They can explain it and describe it well. They are very clever at delivering His Word, causing us to be engaged. But we meet very few, if any anymore, who *tremble* at His Word. The Scriptures, should cause us to tremble. With that being said, it begs to question: How do you view the Scriptures? Do they cause you to tremble? Can you feel the fire of His Spirit coming off of the page at you? Do you think you are capable of trembling at His Word? If so, what will it take to get there?
- As a Christian, would you call yourself hot, cold, or lukewarm? Explain.

A Walking Rebuke

The Sermon on the Mount in Matthew 5-7 is a picture of the true life of the Kingdom of God. In this sermon that Jesus preached, we become acutely aware of our own limitations. It takes us on a journey of our own superficiality. We begin with sackcloth and ashes, then move to salt and light, onward to God's law, then adoration, fear of the Lord, and lastly building our spiritual house. It's beyond our own limited thinking and rationale. It's delivered in a logical, spiritual order concerned with the spiritual life of a Christian and how one regards God's laws. It is all about how His Kingdom operates. We are to "seek first the kingdom of God" and then all things will be added unto us (Matthew 6:33). The temperature of the Church today indicates that we are not doing this. All one must do is read this whole sermon to know we are, in fact, doing the complete opposite.

When Lazarus was raised from the dead, it created something the chief priests could not tolerate. *"Now a great many of the Jews knew that He was there; and they came, not for Jesus' sake only, but that they might also see Lazarus, whom He had raised from the dead. <u>But the chief priests plotted to put Lazarus to death also</u>"* (John 12:9-10). Lazarus was a walking rebuke to the religious authority of that time. He was a testimony to the authority of Christ on the earth. When you are raised from the death of your sins and transferred into the Kingdom of the Son of His love, you pass from death to life, just like Lazarus. And when you live your life fully surrendered to Him, you become a walking rebuke to the kingdom of darkness, testifying of Christ's authority still present on the earth!

In order to be a walking rebuke, our lives must reflect the life of our Redeemer and the miraculous work of moving us from death to life. Jesus Christ is the narrow gate you walked through to pass from death to life. He now becomes the narrow path that you follow to become that walking rebuke to darkness.

In Acts 19:11-16, we read a story of Jewish exorcists who marveled at the authority and power Paul carried when even handkerchiefs and aprons that had touched his body were used to heal the sick in the name of Jesus Christ. They wanted the same power as Paul. They took it upon themselves to try to cast out evil spirits "in the name of Jesus" but it didn't work. The spirits answered and said, "Jesus I know, and Paul I know; but who are you?" Then the spirits leapt on them and overpowered them. These demons knew Jesus and knew Paul because of their power and authority. Both spent time in the secret place of the Most High, the secret place of prayer. They prayed in the power of the Holy Spirit as hell rocked in fury! Their ministry was void of serving themselves and was all about serving the Father.

We cannot just pray a prayer of salvation and think that's it. We have to die to self and let sanctification begin. Dying to self comes in a place of gut-wrenching prayer and surrender of your old nature, maybe for months. Death is not pretty. We have not that power nor authority in our churches yet because we've stopped praying as people who are "poor in spirit." Once we wake up to this truth and get before the throne of God to rid ourselves of ourselves then He'll begin to pour in to us. Believe me, when the body of Christ truly wakes up and begins to pray, the world will know it. You never have to advertise a fire!

Humble and Contrite

What does God command of us? "To love the Lord your God with all your heart and with all of your soul and with all of your strength and with all of your mind" (Luke 10:27). Gideon was a prophet sent by God to remind the Israelites of God's faithfulness, and how the people had nevertheless rejected Him. The Lord sent an angel to visit Gideon and tell him the great things he was going to do. Gideon's reply was "Oh my Lord, how can I save Israel? Indeed, my clan is the weakest in Manasseh, and I am the least in my father's house" (Judges 6:15). Gideon really believed what he said, and he shrank from the very thought of greatness and honor. What does God look for when He calls such a person? "For thus says the High and Lofty One who inhabits eternity, whose name is Holy: 'I dwell in the high and holy place, with him who has a contrite and humble spirit, to revive the spirit of the humble, and to revive the heart of the contrite ones" (Isaiah 57:15).

Merriam Webster's Dictionary defines "contrite" as "feeling or showing sorrow and remorse for a sin or shortcoming." "Humble" means "reflecting, expressing, or offered in a spirit of deference or submission." God looks for sorrow over our sins that comes from reflection and submission. He dwells with the person who has a contrite and humble spirit. Not only that, He "revives" that person. Gideon was such a man, as was Moses, who felt deeply unworthy of the task God called him to. There was also Isaiah who confessed he was a man of unclean lips (Isaiah 6:5), and Jeremiah said, *"Behold, I cannot speak for I am a youth"* (Jeremiah 1:6). The apostles would not dare take a step into the mission fields without first praying and fasting for direction (Acts 13:1-3). Peter, after experiencing a miraculous catch of fish, said, *"Depart from me; for I am a sinful man, O Lord"* (Luke 5:8).

If you want to walk on a different level spiritually, it will require a humble and a contrite heart. It will require repentance. You will have to walk away from distractions in your life, get alone with God, and ask His Spirit to search your heart. It's in that place of aloneness with Him where you feel the conviction of His Spirit upon you. You will not be able to proceed any further in your prayer as He is doing this deep work. It's like an anti-virus software scanning a computer for a virus.

It doesn't take long for the Holy Spirit to search out a virus in you, but sometimes it takes a while to recognize it in ourselves; it's the process of revealing unconfessed sin.

We've become very skilled at not recognizing it anymore because we've learned how to build walls around our hearts. We're very good at hiding things from God. As the Spirit of God searches us, our "viruses" start popping up, evidence that there is something deeply embedded in the fabric of our being that God wants removed. These "viruses" can come in the form of unforgiveness towards someone, offenses, shame, fear, unworthiness, doubt, being judgmental, and countless other things. *"For nothing is secret that will not be revealed, nor anything hidden that will not be known and come to light"* (Luke 8:17). This is why Jesus and the apostles preached repentance before they preached anything else. God is holy and even though He wants to make His holy habitation with you, He will not mix with what is unholy. That is why getting alone with Him is important; it's why He calls it "the secret place."

Every great man God has chosen had to walk alone at some point. You have to lose everything you have to gain everything He has; in other words, you have to lose your life to find it (Matthew 10:39). Are you prepared to do that? *"And no one puts new wine into old wineskins. For the wine would burst the wineskins, and the wine and the skins would both be lost. New wine calls for new wineskins"* (Mark 2:22, NLT). The first thing God requires of you is not to be a missionary or a soul winner. He may use you for that at some point, but the first thing He requires of you is surrender. He wants you to love Him without doing other things first. Your old wine must be poured out; your old self must be destroyed. He wants to create a new wineskin and pour in new wine. However, we are often asking Him to fill us up with something new when we have yet to pour out the old.

Do we want to become the force on the earth that Jesus said the gates of hell would not prevail against? In the days of the early Church, organized religion was able to do nothing for the cripple, who had begged at the gate of the temple called Beautiful so long that everyone knew who he was (Acts 3:1-9). But an outcast preacher, Peter, answered this lame man's need through the Name. If we could rediscover the virtue in that Name, the victory in that Name, the violence (against hell) in that Name, we could set the world alight for God.

But in order to use His Name, He must see our loyalty. No kingdom on earth uses people unless they are first willing to lay down their lives for the crown. Complete allegiance is required, as is knowledge of kingdom law, if one wants to exercise the authority of the Kingdom. That is why the Jewish exorcists who observed Paul's authority could not overcome the evil spirits. They did not belong to the right kingdom; therefore, they could not come in the name of the King.

Make no mistake, spiritual forces of darkness know who walk in God's Kingdom authority. They also know where it's lacking. The Church needs to wake up and know who she is. But for now, we're still playing on the lawn while people perish. God is not concerned about our happiness but about our holiness. If we are the temple of God as He says we are (1 Corinthians 3:16), there is only room for one inside, and He does not share His power. He will use you as a conduit of it, but it's *His* throne set up in your heart, not yours.

I have been in ministry a long time and have had the wonderful privilege of participating in many unique activities, but I found that there is nothing harder than prayer. It's taxing. It takes time. It requires endurance. It denies self and exposes all of our places of vulnerability. And in the Sermon on the Mount, it's the first place Jesus chose to start: *"Blessed are the poor in spirit, for theirs is the kingdom of heaven"* (Matthew 5:3). The Kingdom of Heaven is not for the proud;

it's reserved for those with a contrite and humble spirit. Pride was in the Kingdom once before, and God kicked it out. Jesus said He saw Satan fall like lightning from heaven (Luke 10:18). So, the first stop on the narrow path, and the first step in holiness is to bow low.

Reflect and Respond

- What do you spend most of your time praying about?
- When you leave your house, are you a walking rebuke to the kingdom of darkness? Explain.
- Does hell fear you? Do demons know you like they do Jesus or Paul?
- Think about something or someone in your life that you love with all of your heart and how you show them you love them. Now ask yourself the same thing about God. How do you show God you love Him with all of your heart? With all of your mind? With all of your soul? With all of your strength?
- If you can't answer the previous question, what keeps you from loving Him this way?

Tending to Our Seed

While the world is dying to live, a true Christian should be living to die. John tells us that we become like a grain of wheat that falls into the ground and dies (John 12:24). Unless it dies, it remains by itself, but if it (our self-life) dies, it produces much fruit. Think about everything a seed goes through to produce fruit. First, it gets separated from the main stalk, then it's buried where it lives in a death-like state similar to hibernation. The seed feeds off the husk around it, sustaining it during its first days of growth. Once the seed germinates, it grows into wheat. The wheat is picked, sent to a mill, and put into a threshing machine where it is beaten up so that the chaff comes off and the pure kernel is revealed. Another mill grinds it up into flour, and the flour is kneaded into dough through much pulling and pushing. Finally, it is shaped into bread and baked to be enjoyed by many.

We all start out in seed form and must go into the ground, or alone with God, to die. It's a lonely place to be, but it's necessary. We hibernate with the One who is the true Bread of Life and feed off His sustaining Word. His Word is crucial in the early stages of our growth because it determines if germination will occur or if we'll succumb to environmental pressures. We cannot despise the day of small beginnings. When we begin a new life with Jesus Christ, we want to immediately start being pouring out to others, but we must take care of our seed first and properly tend through its beginning stages of growth so it can produce a bountiful harvest. That's why Jesus shared the parable of the sower:

> Then he told them many things in parables, saying: "A farmer went out to sow his seed. As he was scattering the seed, some fell along the path, and the birds came and ate it up. Some fell on rocky places, where it did not have much soil. It sprang up quickly, because the soil was shallow. But when the sun came up, the plants were scorched, and they withered because they had no root. Other seed fell among thorns, which grew up and choked the plants. Still other seed fell on good soil, where it produced a crop—a hundred, sixty or thirty times what was sown. Whoever has ears, let them hear." (Matthew 13:3-9, NIV)

Jesus then interpreted it:

> Listen then to what the parable of the sower means: When anyone hears the message about the kingdom and does not understand it, the evil one comes and snatches away what was sown in their heart. This is the seed sown along the path. The

> seed falling on rocky ground refers to someone who hears the word and at once receives it with joy. But since they have no root, they last only a short time. When trouble or persecution comes because of the word, they quickly fall away. The seed falling among the thorns refers to someone who hears the word, but the worries of this life and the deceitfulness of wealth choke the word, making it unfruitful. But the seed falling on good soil refers to someone who hears the word and understands it. This is the one who produces a crop, yielding a hundred, sixty or thirty times what was sown. (Matthew 13:18-23, NIV)

This is why the narrow path is important. Jesus goes before us as the One who scatters the seed, and He carefully tends to the soil to make it "good." If we follow Him on this narrow path, our seed will be planted in good soil and produce strong roots and good fruit. He lived 30 years before He went out to work the harvest. Many of us want to reap a harvest without first going through the seed process of cultivating our hearts in order to produce healthy fruit. There are many different levels in the spiritual life, but they all begin in the secret place of the Most High, a place that requires us to be alone. It's hard to be alone. It goes against our nature for many of us and can be our biggest test. But we don't get anywhere unless we get alone first. It's only when God says we're ready, that we can then go forth. Promotion should always come from Him, not from man. Many promotions in Christian circles today are coming from men and not from God. In their eagerness to start or grow a church, they hire from within, promote from within, and then preach from within. Now we have thousands of churches across the country that look the same, sound the same, and do more of the same.

Do you want the will of God to the degree that you are willing to let God take you away to be alone with Him? Moses saw the backside of a wilderness for 40 years before he was sent to Egypt. He could have never faced Pharaoh without that experience. He had grown up living in a palace. For 40 years, he ate, drank, and lived a life of luxury. God couldn't use a "deliverer" from that environment without making some drastic changes first. God had to pluck him out of the palace and stick him in the desert…alone.

Many of us shriek at the mere thought of being alone, yet it's the very training tool He uses to teach us obedience and to hear His voice. David was alone and on the run from Saul for 13 years. Many psalms were birthed during that journey. Paul was alone for three years in Arabia before God used him to write most of the epistles of the New Testament. Elijah was alone during the drought living near a brook before God used him to stand against 450 prophets of Baal and 400 of Asherah. Jesus was alone in the desert before He started His earthly ministry. John was alone on the island of Patmos where he received the revelation of Jesus for the end days.

Don't be afraid of the wilderness! It is there that He refines us. A pulling down must happen before a raising up can begin. He wants to break us and then rebuild us into His likeness. He doesn't want us looking like our old father, the devil, anymore. He wants us looking like Him. It is in the secret place that He destroys the yoke of pride from our life. Only when pride is removed can humility move in.

Reflect and Respond

- Have you ever taken a season of your life to "run away" with God? Not for a day, a week, or a month, but for a season? Schedule one now.
- Schedule one now.

Time to Advance...On Our Knees

The line between the Church and the world is becoming less distinct. There is no one else God has on this earth to advance His Kingdom but us. He could have cleared out the angelic hosts of heaven to do this work, but He didn't. He chose us. The seed is the Word and must be sown in our hearts before it can fructify. Then, and only then, can we bear it to others. Paul tells us to "be no longer children," because children bear their kind. The mature bring about reproduction. I'm afraid we're still children producing children because the Word of God is not sown in our hearts.

According to the American Bible Institute, the average American family has 3.5 Bibles in their homes. With that many Bibles, one would assume we are all well versed in Scripture. Unfortunately, that is not the case.

God is looking for people to stand in the gap for a lost world. This position is not entrusted to the immature, but we have become so limited in our doctrinal circles. We're on a treadmill of having *"the appearance of wisdom"* (Colossians 2:23) and can't get off, *"ever learning and never able to come to the knowledge of truth"* (2 Timothy 3:7, KJV). When 911 happened, people sprinted for the house of God. Many thought the fire of revival had come. Six short weeks later, we were back to our same complacency, and like the church at Sardis, thinking we were alive and well when we were and are, according to God's perspective, dead (Revelation 3:1)

Our nation is sick, and the cause of the disease upon it is spiritual. People are not your enemy; the devil is your enemy. He roams this earth as a roaring lion to see who he may devour. Once he finds them—those seed with no spiritual root—he sends in his dark servants to do the dirty work. There is no organization nor man or woman on the face of the earth that will be able to save us except the person of Jesus Christ. Our salvation lies in Him alone, and until we become a nation under Him, we will continue to buy the bag of goods every snake oil salesman will sell us. No amount of money in the world will buy us out of this mess. We must come to the knowledge of truth, get on our knees, and beg for mercy.

Only God and His Church upon the earth—faithful believers in Jesus Christ—have the answer for the problems that plague us. But until we get positioned on our knees rather than our behinds, that answer will have to wait. We speak of humility but groan when we're overlooked. We speak of the cross but know nothing of fasting. We write about prayer, teach about prayer and preach on prayer but do as little of it as we can. We're fooling no one but ourselves. Our churches are stylish, but services are cold. We have fog machines but no fire. It's our own self that hinders revival and sabotages prayer.

God will not use the man that promotes himself. He will use the man who is wandering around the desert looking for a lost sheep and then reveal Himself in a burning bush or the woman who visits the temple day in and day out covering the floor in tears as she begs God for a child. He will use your friend who spends years in prayer on behalf of a wayward child. Although her heart cries to be out in the mission field of the younger generation, God has kept her in a secret place of prayer, a place of anguish and surrender. These are the people God is ready to use. These are the people who will usher in revival. These are the people whose seed will germinate and produce a harvest. God is looking for the person who is poor in spirit—the person who recognizes his own smallness but says, *"Here am I! Send me"* (Isaiah 6:8). He's looking for you.

"Blessed are the poor in spirit, for theirs is the kingdom of heaven."

Practical Practices

Chapter 2

Church

Write your findings in a journal or notepad.

Observe the atmosphere of your church this week. Is there fear of the Lord? Is there holiness? Is the fire of the Holy Spirit noticeable? Did you worship the Lord in the beauty of holiness, as per the previous video teaching?

Home

Practice praying in a posture of submission to God this week, on your knees if you are able or flat on the floor.

Being humble and contrite is recognizing our sin, mourning over it, and humbling ourselves before God. For your prayer times this week (and after) begin by asking Him to search your heart for any unconfessed sin and start pouring out your confession as He leads. Picture old wine being poured out. Write down what sin(s) He shows you, renounce them (like taking scissors and cutting off any agreements you have made with that sin), and then repent of those sins.

Next, observe your feelings towards your sins. Journal what you find yourself feeling, if anything. Do this every day this week.

From here on out, make it a daily practice to ask God to search your heart for any unconfessed sin.

Read

Write down what the Holy Spirit reveals to you about yourself and God in the following verses:

- Read Joel 3:14.
- Read Deuteronomy 18:10-12.
- Read Isaiah 46:5-13 and 47:12-15.
- Read Colossians 3-4.
- Read 1 John 1:5-10.
- Read Ecclesiastes 5:1-3 and 12:13-14.

Listen

- "Samuel's Awakening" by Jason Upton, *Open Up the Earth*
- "As in the Days of Noah" by Misty Edwards, *Always on His Mind*
- "Empty My Soul" by Jonathan David & Melissa Helser, *Endless Ocean, Bottomless Sea*

CHAPTER 3

BLESSED ARE THOSE WHO MOURN

"Because they have forsaken Me and made this an alien place, because they have burned incense in it to other gods whom neither they, their fathers, nor the kings of Judah have known, and have filled this place with the blood of the innocents."

— JEREMIAH 19:4

A professing Christian stands out from the rest of the world. Everything God teaches us to do is an expression of who He is and flies in the face of the world's standards of living. Consider the following Scriptures: *"He who finds his life will lose it, and he who loses his life for My sake will find it* (Matthew 10:39); *"And whoever exalts himself will be humbled, and he who humbles himself will be exalted"* (Matthew 23:12); *"To live is Christ, and to die is gain"* (Philippians 1:21); *"It is more blessed to give than to receive"* (Acts 20:35). We're a walking contradiction to the world, and the world does not know what to do with us.

God is not looking for supermen or superwomen, He's looking for weak men or women, those who are surrendered and poured out, those who look upon themselves and can't imagine how God can use someone like them. It's in that place of weakness when He is strong, and because everything that God does is contrary to the world, we must come to realize that we too will be contrary to the world when we follow Him.

Our journey on the narrow path through the narrow gate is a spiritual journey. It follows the spiritual laws of God's Kingdom and has nothing to do with the natural life in this world. That's why it's so hard for us to follow Christ on this path. That's why few find it. It's goes against human nature. We have to take the first blessed step of dying to our old nature and becoming poor in spirit, pouring out old wine, before God can pour in. We must start decreasing before He begins increasing in our lives. It's a "good" negative before a positive, just like how conviction precedes conversion.

What the Church is failing to recognize today is the fact that many of us do not have our own personal spiritual houses in order. As a result, we grow weary of trying to figure out God's plan for our lives. We burn out after years of dedicating our lives to serving Him and become frustrated when we keep sliding back into old sin patterns. It's not just ourselves; pastors, priests, and laymen are doing the best they can with what they know, but they, too, get depleted and then their spiritual house is out of order. As the head goes, so goes the body.

We spend so much time figuring out how to reach the lost, but history shows us that when there is a fire lit within the Church itself, meaning you and me, people are naturally drawn to its light. They are curious if this whole Christianity thing is the real deal. Many people are weary, lost, alone, and hurting; they want to know they can truly hope in something and would love to find a place that offers the solution. They don't know it's Jesus Christ crucified. But because God's fire is out—or maybe it's a small flicker—in many churches and believers, people are searching elsewhere for the answers.

That is why we must start with ourselves, the *ekklesia*, the church. To carry the compassion Jesus had, we have to start from the beginning. We must yield to the Holy Spirit and ask Him to *"search me, O God, and know my heart; try me, and know my anxieties; and see if there is any wicked way in me, and lead me in the way everlasting*" (Psalm 139:23-24). This brings us to the next spiritual law Jesus gives us in the Sermon on the Mount: *"Blessed are those who mourn, for they shall be comforted"* (Matthew 5:4).

Again, it's the "good" negative before the positive. We must all be convicted of sin before we can experience the true joy of salvation. Mourning begins in surrender. It's not a worldly mourning but mourning in the very depths of our being. When we choose to come into the wilderness with God, we come face to face with our sinfulness. Aloneness causes us to meditate not just on sin itself but reflect on why these sins rule over us to begin with. Aloneness ushers in self-examination and in that self-examination, we become aware of who we truly are. We begin to ask ourselves important questions: Why can't I forgive that person? What is it in me that makes me behave like that? Why did I go into a fit of rage? Why am I jealous or unkind? Why do I enjoy gossip so much? Why won't my filthy language leave me? What can't I overcome, Lord? Help! *"O wretched man that I am! Who will deliver me from this body of death?"* (Romans 7:24).

We become so grief stricken about ourselves that we mourn. Christians do not like to be acquainted with grief. We try to assume a kind of happiness, which is not something that rises from within, but is something which is put on (like putting on a happy face). There's superficiality about it in order to cut out a certain figure for ourselves.

We're all guilty of it at some time or other. We want to look pious or holy in front of other Christians because, in our mind, it quietly confirms we're on the right track with God. But the *joy of the Lord* rises from within and is the thing that determines our appearance and behaviors regardless of our circumstances. To achieve this place of joy, we must first learn what it feels like to grieve over the ugliness of sin. We'll never understand how to serve the world until we understand how much God detests sin, in ourselves and in mankind in general.

Reflect and Respond

- Get into a quiet place and take a mirror. Stare into your reflection for two minutes. Describe the kind of person you see.
- Ask the Holy Spirit to show you the ugliness of sin and why it grieves God. Write what He shows you.
- If Jesus visited you today in person and asked you to name the very thing in the world that you would love to do in service for Him, what would it be?
- Discuss this with Him in prayer.

Man of Sorrows

When we "die daily," we invite self-examination. We mourn over the wounds inflicted upon us or the ones we inflicted upon others, either years ago or yesterday. We mourn as we pour out because we stare directly into what came out. It works like a mirror, and we find ourselves looking at our own wretchedness. Oh, wretched person that I am because…I stole Your glory at church today, because I turned to the bottle again, because I gossiped or publicly shamed them, because I overruled my husband today or cursed my boss, because I haven't had the strength to forgive, because…

The examination is worse than your annual doctor visit because it doesn't end. Then the realization hits us: Why would You die on a cross for someone like me? And there we have it…the beginning to the end of self. Every day, we must live a life of surrender because sin crouches at the door waiting for us to forfeit our lives to it once again. We must look into the mirror of His Word so that His Word discovers our condition because every day, we are at war within ourselves. But as hard as it is, God considers it a blessing: *"Blessed are those who mourn, for they shall be comforted"* (Matthew 5:4).

As we're mourning over our sin, something new comes forth: a sorrow birthed from God's own heart, a mourning for others. Something transfers. Rather than focusing on ourselves, we suddenly find ourselves caring about others. Not that we didn't care before, but this is something new. It's deeper. The eyes of our heart are opening, scanning the earth, and we find ourselves crying out for the lost, the persecuted, the imprisoned. We start feeling supernatural compassion and anguish for the lost souls of the world. We ache for our enemies, society, and other nations. We can no longer watch television, surf our computers, or read things without looking at them through a different lens entirely. We begin to mourn for the world, just as Jesus did. We mourn over the hateful, stubborn, proud dispositions of people. We mourn over rebellion, idolatry, evil, greed, the lies, and the overall destruction that the enemy spews out over the earth, and we cry out. *"Adonai, there is no one like You to help in battle between the mighty and the powerless. Help us, Adonai Eloheinu, for we rely on You and in Your Name we have come against this multitude. You are Adonai Eloheinu! Let no man prevail against You"* (2 Chronicles 14:11, TLV).

The state of mankind becomes an ache in our heart. We see the sin and mourn because of it. That is why Jesus was called a *"man of sorrows and acquainted with grief"* (Isaiah 53:3). He wept over

Lazarus because death was never in the plan of creation. He wept over Jerusalem's rejection of Him because He knew judgment was about to come. It's part of His nature to mourn, and His nature must emerge in us if we are to walk this narrow path with Him. If we are not mourning the things that He mourns for, it begs to question if we have His nature in us. We ask for signs, wonders, and miracles to be done through us. We want worship we can jump up and down to. We want sermons to carry us through our week, our job, our marriage, our struggles, our pain. But we don't want to become acquainted with grief.

Blessed are those who mourn because we are receiving His nature in us. The true intention and interpretation of this verse is to build upon the laws of the Kingdom Jesus is setting forth here. Sin entered the world and brought with it terrible results. We mourn because we see the results of sin all around us, and God has given us an understanding of what sin meant to Him. He hates it. It stabs Him in the heart. He allows us to feel that stabbing pain in the hopes we not only mourn it but desire to do something about it. It's in the mourning where compassion is birthed, and once birthed, we can bring the gospel of the Kingdom to people much easier because He has allowed us to feel His heart towards them, no matter who it is. This is what mourning means in the spiritual sense. The Sermon on the Mount is not just a teaching or sermon, but a spiritual journey. We tend to look at the Beatitudes from the perspective of their physical fulfillment when they were intended to be a journey of the heart.

Reflect and Respond

This week try to explore the following organizations and journal if God shows you something new about His heart for the world.

- The Voice of the Martyrs: search "Prisoner Alerts," then click on "Prisoners" and read their stories.

- World Watch Monitor, worldwatchmonitor.org
- Christian Solidarity International Twitter Feed: https://twitter.com/CSI_USA
- Ex-Muslim TV Twitter Feed, read Muslim testimonies: https://twitter.com/ExMuslimTV
- I Met Messiah, read Jewish testimonies: https://www.oneforisrael.org/met-messiah-jewish- testimonies/

The Comforter

The Lord finishes this statement on mourning with an encouragement: those that mourn will be comforted. What a paradox! If we mourn, we'll become happy? That doesn't seem natural, but then again, the gospel of His Kingdom is *super*natural, so of course, it doesn't make sense to our natural minds. Our hearts are now maturing, and pride is losing its home. Our focus in prayer is evolving, and we're taking on His focus—what matters to Him. We take comfort that Christ is the answer to this life. He is the perfect provision for not only us but the world. This becomes a reality for us.

No longer we will wonder how to share the gospel with someone or be angry when someone disagrees with us or hate a terrorist who bombs a church. Because God is sharing His heart with us, we see that Jesus is the only answer for the terrorist, the greedy businessman, or the cheating spouse. We feel His ache in us which makes us a more determined witness for His gospel because, like Him, we desire that none should perish but that all should come to a place of repentance and recognize Jesus as their answer. Fear leaves us because compassion takes over. Are you beginning to see why we have to start with the journey to holiness before anything else? We'll fear sharing the gospel otherwise.

The answer to this world is not the next great evangelist or the next great politician. Jesus is the only answer the world is seeking. He is not the same God over all the religions of the world despite what the world tells you. He's unique, He's narrow, and He says that the world will know us by our fruit. We have got to get alone with God so that He can work on our seed and reveal truth to us. That fresh outpouring of understanding brings tremendous comfort. Your great sorrow leads to joy and will continue throughout your Christian life as you grow in Him.

I absolutely love this verse in Scripture, and especially in this translation: *"I am convinced that any suffering we endure is less than nothing compared to the magnitude of glory that is about to be unveiled within us. The entire universe is standing on tiptoe, yearning to see the unveiling of God's glorious sons and daughters"* (Romans 8:18-19, TPT). There is an intense anticipation in heaven of what we are going to look like when Jesus comes for His bride. The Church will not look like what you see now. A complete transformation must occur, and the Holy Spirit is at the helm of that transformation. Scripture says that no one can come to the Son unless first drawn by the Father. Once we recognize the Son, the Holy Spirit begins His ever-important job of transforming us into His image.

Think about who Jesus was and what He did, and you will see His life in the Sermon on the Mount. The Eternal left heaven…for us. No wonder being poor in spirit is such a critical first step. Are you willing to leave what this world offers and surrender your life to His leading, which looks contrary to the world you left? Are you willing to let Him break your heart for what breaks His?

The writer of the book of Hebrews tells us that everything that can be shaken will be shaken. Why? To usher in His unshakable Kingdom. Look at the governments of the world being shaken. Look at Hollywood being shaken. Look at God's Church being shaken. He is disrupting the worlds systems to open our eyes. He will expose corruption, fornication, lewdness, greed, and the like to show us that everything we used to put our hope in will fail us. He doesn't want you to comfort yourself in these things anymore. He is our only source of hope and strength and. must become the Comforter to you.

The state of the world should cause you to mourn, not because of losing "the good ole days," but because of the evidence of sin's intense destruction in the lives of people. But there is comfort for those who seek His face. We know there is a glory that yet remains. Even though we groan in prayer, we rejoice in the blessed hope of our King's return. Our ultimate hope should not be resolving global warming or famine but in gaining eternity. Dr. Martin Lloyd Jones describes what we have to look forward to: "In that eternal state, we shall be wholly and entirely blessed, there will be nothing to mar life, nothing to detract from it, nothing to spoil it. Sorrow and sighing shall be no more; all tears will be wiped away; and bliss and glory unmixed and unspoiled."

The Power of the Gospel

What we are missing in the church today is a true sorrow over sin. Repentance was always the first step in everything Jesus did. Jesus gave His disciples power over unclean spirits and sent them out two by two but note what they preached: *"So they went out and preached that people should repent"* (Mark 6:12). Today we hear it preached that "the battle has already been won at Calvary." We relax and our hand goes off the wheel; we look doe-eyed to the front of a church for man to steer our cruise ship safely to shore. Christ did triumph over the enemy and over sin, but that does not eliminate our human responsibility. It is time to comprehend the cross of Christ because a time is coming, and is already here, where people will not endure sound doctrine. Every gimmick-geared gospel we hear today would fall flat in Rome during the days of Paul. Here's a man who measured the might of Calvary with every step he took. He watched thousands, and tens of thousands, leaving the coliseum, jubilant that once more Christians had provided exciting entertainment for them and an excellent meal for lions! Can you imagine standing outside of one our football stadiums watching tens of thousands of people exiting in pure elation at the sport of killing Christians?

Sadly, we're moving in that direction. Currently, we are taking sides in a climate of hate. It's become sport to see who has the sharpest tongue of rebuke, the cleverest banter designed to humiliate, or the rudest gesture in order to silence. We have become pawns in this game of chess between light and darkness. We better be very clear on whose side we want to be on. Paul was. He didn't arrive in Rome admiring the architecture and grandiose nature of the coliseum. No, he came on the scene with weighted words and the banner of Christ held high. He came against pagan parties and wicked hoards with power and authority boldly declaring, "I AM NOT ASHAMED OF THE GOSPEL OF CHRIST FOR IT IS THE POWER OF GOD TO SALVATION" (Romans 1:16).

There is one thing that keeps us from complete decay in this hour—the Church, the true Church, the blood-washed remnant that has not bowed its knee to the god of materialism and cannot be intimidated by the threats and scorn of modern-day humanism. The true Church is a people like Paul, not ashamed of the gospel of Christ, not ashamed to stand in the gap and offer prayers on behalf of what grieves God, a church that is humble enough to mourn over sin.

No world leader can divert a divine plague; only repentance by a broken and a contrite church can do that. And, my friends, the plagues are coming. The end of the age is upon us. We better learn how to pray and how to yield. Things are going to develop rapidly, more rapidly than you can anticipate. There is no better time than right now to get right with God. We need to wake up and stand up and begin pulling down the altars we're building to Baal and Ashtoreth. They were gods of the Old Testament that were an abomination to God; they're still an abomination to God now because those same spirits are still active in the world today. In our slumber, the spirit of the Antichrist has sown division, confusion, offense, death, and destruction across our land.

Whether you're pro-life or pro-choice, God grieves over the death of 60 million babies murdered through abortion in the United States alone since the passing of Roe vs. Wade in 1973. That's ten times the Jewish Holocaust of WWII! Our schools today are no different than those in Russia; no Bibles, no prayer, no crosses, no baccalaureates, no prayer on the football field or at graduations, and no reference to Christmas. Yet, we welcome the five pillars of Islam, the Hindu sikhs, Buddha, mindfulness, and after school yoga classes.

These things should grieve us because they grieve God. These two things alone should stir us to repentance for fear of His judgments upon our nation. We can label them anything we want, but they are sin. Jesus said, *"He who is not with Me is against Me"* (Matthew 12:30). Nehemiah and Daniel repented for and mourned for the sins of their nation, and God heard their cry. Never underestimate the power of sorrowful repentance and the grace that flows from mourning. The Holy Spirit is called the Comforter because when all hope seems lost, we have His blessed assurance. He does not shout His secrets over a loud speaker; rather, He whispers them in the secret place.

"Blessed are those who mourn, for they will be comforted."

PRACTICAL PRACTICES

CHAPTER 3

Day to Day

Write your findings in a journal or notepad.

Keep a journal with you at all times this week. Write down as many situations you come across, in person, on the news, at work, etc. that you believe would grieve God. Keep a thorough list.

Home

Pray over the list you are compiling every day. After your time of emptying, confess the things on your list that you believe grieve the Lord. Repent for them. We're all part of one body, so though we may not be personally guilty of certain sins, like Daniel and Nehemiah, we should confess corporate, national sins as well as individual sins.

Thank Him for allowing you to notice these things that grieve Him.

Create some type of a prayer wall, bulletin board, or notebook to keep a regular log of things you believe He wants you to keep "front and center" in prayer. God is good about sharing the burdens of His heart throughout His body of praying believers so no one feels overwhelmed. He doesn't expect you to cover it all, but He might give you a specific assignment (person, school, church, business, politician, country, etc.). Make it a priority to pray over that particular matter, whether it's continual repentance or whatever it is He shows you.

Read

Meditate on these verses about the compassion of God:

- Read Genesis 18:16-19:29.
- Read Nehemiah 1-2.
- Read Daniel 9:3-19 (then re-read with the name of your nation and people in it).
- Read Luke 7:11-17 (note Jesus' compassion)
- Read Mark 5:1-20 (note Jesus' compassion)
- Read Matthew 10:35-38 (note Jesus' compassion)

Listen

- "Streams of Mercy" by Joel Chernoff, *The Best of Messianic Praise & Worship*
- "Mercy Seat" by Travis Cottrell & Angela Cruz, *Jesus Saves*
- "Speak to Me" by Kari Jobe, *The Garden*
- "Teach Me How to Pray" by Jason Upton, *Sunday Morning Live in Winston Salem*

CHAPTER 4

Blessed Are the Meek

"Do not love the world or the things in the world. If anyone loves the world, the love of the Father is not in him. For all that is in the world—the lust of the flesh, the lust of the eyes, and the pride of life—is not of the Father but is of the world. And the world is passing away, and the lust of it; but he who does the will of God abides forever."

— 1 John 2:15-17

I'll never forget when he walked into the room. He walked in quietly with his wife and humbly introduced himself, "I'm Pastor Lee." It was the National Day of Prayer, and a group of us were hosting an event in our little town nestled in the foothills of Colorado. It was a miracle how God connected the two of us together. Through a mutual acquaintance at my local dry cleaners, this precious Korean pastor, who lived across the city, graciously accepted our invitation to lead a prayer for the nations on this day. He drove an hour to our town because, according to him, "Father" told him to come.

Prayer had been taking place all day. A schedule had been carefully crafted, and the crowds ebbed and flowed based on particular prayer topics. Pastor Lee was scheduled over the lunch hour. There were just a handful of us present as we took our seats and he approached the front of the room. Pastor Lee walked up to the tiny platform, turned to the wall, removed his shoes, and knelt on the floor. What came next hit me to the core. A cry of intercession proceeded from this man from nowhere else but deep places within his spirit. In an instant, an ache filled my soul because I knew what I was hearing was an ache from God Himself coming through this man.

Those of us in the room could not resist the anointing that came. We got out of our seats and onto the floor, and our spirits joined his in holy abandon. It was like casting our crowns before the King. The sins of the nations required repentance, and we felt the pain of God's heart for His people. All we could do was bear that pain until prayer was birthed into the spirit realm. A day is coming when the answer to that prayer will be poured out from the bowls of heaven.

When Pastor Lee finished, he wiped his eyes, stood up, put his shoes back on his feet, quietly came down off the platform, and walked to the back of the room. He did nothing to bring attention to himself. We stood up, wiping our own tears away, thanking him for such an incredible prayer of intercession. He responded by giving God all the glory. He thanked us for the invitation and considered it such a privilege. We were the ones who felt privileged, yet he kept telling us how much we had blessed him. Then he and wife invited us to come to their church so they could cook us a real Korean meal, and we could pray and worship together! We accepted the invitation, and within a couple of weeks, that's exactly what we were doing. Dinner turned into laughter, laughter turned into worship, and then worship turned into deep intercessory prayer.

I left there knowing there was something very important missing in my Christian life. I wanted God's heart to live in me the way it so obviously lived in this man. Since then a friendship has formed. This man of God is someone few people have heard of in Christian circles, but he is well known in the realms of heaven. He's a poured-out vessel, empty of self and serving the Lord day and night. He does not take days off, for he knows the time is short upon the earth, and he commits himself to the work of the Lord. He mourns deeply for lost souls and spends his time serving the poor, training up pastors, and leading his own congregation. The people follow his lead, and they too are poured-out vessels, praying without ceasing and growing in the knowledge of God. He knows what it takes to walk the narrow path. He has surrendered, emptied himself, and mourns over sin. It is no wonder this man possesses the incredible attribute of meekness.

Contemporary preaching and soulish praying cater to the flesh, while biblical teaching and Spirit-led prayer crucifies the flesh. These bid you to come and die. The Beatitudes rise one above the other like the rungs on a ladder, and those that come before are always necessary to those that follow after. When a man is converted, the first operation of God's grace within his soul is true poverty of spirit that makes us know our weakness and humbles us. Next, He makes us mourn over our deficiencies that are so manifest in us. First, there is a true knowledge of ourselves and then a sacred grief.

No man can truly be meek until he first knows himself. Meekness is evidence of the work of the Holy Spirit within him. While the first two steps deal primarily with personal examination, meekness is designed to be geared more towards our fellow man. He's not just meek within himself, but his meekness is manifest in his dealings with others.

We live in a world that has lost its way and in a church that has lost its voice. Many people have no idea what it means to carry the attributes of God or to "be holy for I am holy." We don't know what to do with a man like Pastor Lee because we're so used to big personalities on big stages or used to rituals and rote prayers, both of which look nothing like the early Church. Meekness is not attractive to today's glossy world of Christianity. If a Christian conference was being held down the street, there's a good chance its keynote speakers would be well-known men and women.

What would a conference like that do if they invited a man like Pastor Lee to speak? What if he walked to the stage, took off his shoes, turned his back from the crowd of thousands, faced the wall, and cried in intercession for an hour? I'll tell you what they would do—fall on the floor! When meekness enters in, pride walks out. When the Holy Spirit is given the stage, the fire falls. And these people, expecting to have their feet washed and plates filled, are instead witnessing a man who no longer views himself worthy of anything except washing the feet of Jesus. A man like that, who is intimate with God, is not intimidated by anyone.

Reflect and Respond

- Ponder what you believe it looks like to be meek. Now examine your own life. As a follower of Jesus Christ, in what ways does the world see meekness in you?
- If you can't think of any, ask God to show you how meekness *could* look in your life.
- Try something different in your prayer time this week: maybe remove your shoes, kneel down, face a wall. Take another step in coming out of your comfort zone.

Watchman Arise

Meekness is sorely needed in our Christian walk. It does not mean being isolated or becoming a monk. It's a virtue, a spiritual attribute of God. It reveals itself in the person who goes lower and lower still, while society goes higher and higher. We need to learn how to walk through the eye of the needle. Are we willing to lay down our confidence, our spiritual gifts, talents, and personal ambitions and walk through the tiny entry point the needle offers? We have to learn not to depend on ourselves. On the other side, we find that Jesus is there waiting to hand us back our spiritual gifts, talents, and ambitions. He points the way to the narrow path and says. "Well done, faithful servant. Now, keep walking."

It's time to lay down our spiritual crutches and walk. We have depended on them too much, which means we're not depending enough on God. He wants us to learn how to stand and be strong in Him. Things are coming upon the earth that we are not ready for; many are already here. Most of us do to know how to stand on the Word of God or in the strength of the Holy Spirit. At the first sign of tribulation, we will be consumed. To prepare His disciples for all that was to follow the Last Supper—three days of utter confusion, turmoil, and testing—Jesus told them the parable of the Vine and the Branches.

This lesson is likewise for us, who will traverse the final great trial of this age. *"If you abide in Me, and My words abide in you, you will ask what you desire, and it shall be done for you. By this My Father is glorified, that you bear much fruit; so you will be My disciples"* (John 15:7-8). We must learn how to abide.

Meekness is cultivated in us as we learn to die daily to self. It is in meekness when we begin to abide. Abiding means that you endure while continually yielding. You learn to wait on the Lord. Your eyes move off of you and remain stable and fixed on Him. Abiding in Him teaches you patience with others, and Christian forbearance becomes a quality noticed by the world because it is missing in the world. Meekness must be exercised before we can move further in our journey down the narrow path.

God's going to give us a new breed of men and women, of all ages. He's been waking up the watchman, those who will discern the times, stand guard, and blow the trumpet to warn others to wake up. Are you willing to be a watchman? It means living a crucified life and being set on fire by God Himself. You will not hold your peace, nor your prayers day and night, nor have rest. You will be a poured-out vessel called to walk in humility, kindness, and gentleness but in the power and authority of Jesus Christ. Do you want that? He's calling those people right now. He's calling you.

At the judgment seat of Christ, there will be too many of us who God may say "Son, daughter, I had many things to tell you, but you couldn't bear them. You were too occupied. Your ears were catching other voices, not Mine." My friends, I pray that our ears are tuned to the frequency of the Spirit, and that we do not miss our day of visitation when He asks us to join the battle. It is time to put away childish things: *"When I was a child, I spoke as a child, I understood as a child, I thought as a child; but when I became a man, I put away childish things"* (1 Corinthians 13:11).

Reflect and Respond

- Examine the current state of your Christian life. What things are childish? What things are mature?
- In prayer, ask God how you can put away the childish things. Ask how to grow from there so that you can become a "watchman on the wall" in the place He's assigned you.

To Be Known by God, Not by Men

Pastor Lee had one thing on his mind that day, ministering to his Lord. He acknowledged God's holiness by removing his shoes and kneeling on the floor. When he faced the wall, he was acknowledging that it wasn't about him, and then he proceeded to pour forth oil. We must never forget who it is who sits on that throne of grace we're coming so boldly towards. There's a scene in heaven around that throne of grace that, were we to witness in person, would cause us to fall down as though dead. It's hard to picture that kind of holiness because it doesn't exist here on earth, so we have nothing to compare it to. But when you're with God in the secret place of prayer, He gives us a glimpse into that kind of holiness because *"He who dwells in the secret place of the Most High shall abide under the shadow of the Almighty* (Psalm 91:1). We abide under His shadow and draw nourishment and secrets from the Vine.

A few years after meeting Pastor Lee, I reached out to him about another prayer event. We exchanged some notes back and forth, and in one of his replies, he wanted to share with me what God was doing in Peru. He made no mention of what his church was doing in Peru, just what *God* was doing there. The mission, birthed by long hours of prayer, was to free 50,000 children from desperation and pain and fill them with joy and peace from a new life in Christ. I watched the video he sent me with admiration at the obedience of these people to listen to and follow the will of God. They live a life of abiding which is why God can trust them with His work upon the earth.

There is so much to be done, and we can't keep coming back to the chorale week in and week out expecting food to be waiting in the trough. That food needs to start going somewhere. As a result of their obedience in Peru, not only did 50,000 children get blessed, but God helped this team erect the largest tent in the history of Peru to be built for worship. He knew He could entrust that task with an abiding man.

The meek are submissive to God's will and flexible to His Word. Whatever God wills, they will. They learn to hold things loosely and forfeit control. They learn to bend to His will, while surrendering theirs, and become pliable in His hands. They come to know that they are the least of all saints, and in some respects, the chief of all sinners. The meek no longer seek the best seat at the feast or the best church on the block in which to build their own kingdom. Their behavior indicates that they consider themselves debtors to the loving kindness of the Lord.

I worked with a man at a church who was in charge of facilities management. He was a quiet man, always walking through the buildings cleaning up after everyone. He was humble and gentle in spirit, and never once did I hear him complain. While the "movers and shakers" of the church received the glory, he got the backaches. One day as he and I were talking outside about the leadership's desire to expand and how his role might change, he said to me, "Carole, if God just has me sweep the floors in His Kingdom, I would be happy." His comment has stuck with me all these years later. He just wants to be near his King, even if he's sweeping the floors. How many of us can say that? While many vie for teaching positions and leadership roles in organizations or just long to be noticed in some of the ways we serve Christ, this man is already miles ahead of them because his attitude is like the psalmist's: *"I would rather be a doorkeeper in the house of my God than dwell in the tents of the wicked"* (Psalm 84:10).

Are you beginning to understand what I'm telling you? Is God—just Him—going to be enough for you? If all He asked of you from now until the day you leave this earth was to be alone with Him in prayer and stop all your other endeavors, would that be okay with you? Would just being with Him be enough?

The Holy Spirit is looking for a body to dwell in to birth the purposes of God upon the earth. No wonder it comes after poverty in spirit and mourning. When we are meek, we are no longer over sensitive to ourselves and self-interests. What a curse we put upon ourselves!

What a curse I put upon myself for years—this sensitivity to self. I spent so much time worrying about what people thought: Did I upset them? Did I say something wrong? Did they misunderstand me? Am I doing what you want me to do Lord? We can spend our whole lives watching ourselves but when a meek man comes along, we see that he's finished with all of that; he no longer worries about himself or what other people say. Such a person realizes that no one can harm you. If fact, you're amazed that God would choose to use you at all.

Reflect and Respond

- Watch "ABBA PERU 2014": https://www.youtube.com/watch?v=GOZ0ZGDZXQk
- Are you crippled by how people view you? Does it limit you sharing the gospel of Christ with others? Are you afraid of offending them?
- Is God enough for you? If He hides you away in the secret place from now until you leave this earth, and people rarely saw you, would a life with Him like that satisfy you?

Inheriting the Earth

There are many of us today who no longer go to the house of God to meet God; we go to the house of God to hear a sermon about God. We are wondering why God does not move while He is wondering why we do not break. We are more impressed by the brilliant man who can answer all our questions than by the devout man who stumbles over his replies. We are even tempted to swallow almost any piece of information as long as its backed up by the "experts." There are "fashions" in theology just as there are clothes, and quite a few are unrelated to divine truth and human need. This is why the Beatitudes are essential. They are your guidepost to the spiritual laws of God's Kingdom. They will never steer you to the wide path of destruction.

That is why the meek will inherit the earth. They enjoy what they have whether it's a lot or a little. They enjoy where God sends them, whether to many or to few. They live in a place of contentment, expecting nothing but see that spiritually they are being given everything. They want nothing more but to see God's glory fill the earth. This inheriting of the earth became manifest in front of me during a prayer event in our city's capitol.

An older gentleman approached me with an opportunity to bring people into the dome of the Capitol building to pray. He gave me a set time to do this and his phone number to call him when we were ready. I had a very small window to work with and was eager to gather people for this assignment, but as I looked around, everyone had scattered for lunch. I asked God to help and bring the ones whose eyes were fixed on Him and hearts were bent to Your will. Within ten minutes, the area was flooded with 25 of the meekest yet mightiest prayer warriors I know, few of whom knew each other, and among them, Pastor Lee. The meek inherited this assignment and went up into the dome praying down strongholds over our city and state. When finished, these meek ones were wiping away tears and speaking of nothing but the glory of God.

I want to be ready. I don't want to have a lukewarm heart or a lukewarm walk. I want a heart on fire for the simple reason He's coming for a bride, not a widow. If you don't keep a fire burning, it goes out, but if God is that fire—and He is a consuming fire—and He takes up residence in you, you burn till you die. That's how I want to live. I want to see the prayer altars in our hearts ignited once again so that we die to self *"for to me, to live is Christ and to die is gain"* (Philippians

1:21). I want to be chosen for Kingdom assignments and live to give Him the glory due His name.

Through the fire of His Spirit set ablaze in our hearts, the meek really will inherit the earth. He's calling us for such a time as this. It's time to find our lives and let the walls down and the fire in. Walk to the platform, take off your shoes, face the wall, and get on your knees. Do not come down off of your watchman wall until He has birthed a prayer in you for a people He loves, for God's portion is His people, and He will go to great lengths for His kids.

"Blessed are the meek, for they shall inherit the earth."

PRACTICAL PRACTICES
CHAPTER 4

Day to Day

Write your findings in a journal or notepad.

For one week make conversations with strangers everywhere you go, even if it's inconvenient. Ask them as much as possible about themselves. Show a genuine interest. Ask them their name and if they would mind you praying for them this week? Journal what you discovered. Now try to make this a habit.

Home

What is your attitude towards your enemies? What is your attitude towards people who think differently than you politically, socially, or spiritually? Pray for your heart towards these people to change. Ask God to give you His heart for them. Reach out to them over the next week to just tell them you were thinking about them.

This next act of meekness may be incredibly difficult for you, but one that is guaranteed to touch the heart of God. Wash the feet of someone this week. Yes, you heard correctly, wash someone's feet. If you are married, wash your spouse's feet and anoint them with oil afterwards, if you have anointing oil, otherwise just use lotion. If you are not married, carefully decide whose feet the Lord would want you to wash. Washing someone's feet is a deep act of love and submission.

Read

Meditate on these verses on the compassion of God:

- Read Numbers 12:3.
- Read 2 Corinthians 10:1-1.
- Read James 3:13-4:17.
- Read Ecclesiastes 7:1-15, 21.
- Read Jeremiah 38:5-13 and Lamentations 3:46-58.

Listen

- "I Will Exalt" by Amanda Falk, *Bethel Live: Be Lifted High*
- "I Exalt Thee" by Chris Quilala, *Jesus Culture, Your Love Never Fails*
- "I AM, 365 Names of God" by John Paul Jackson

CHAPTER 5

Blessed Are Those Who Hunger and Thirst

"Behold, I stand at the door and knock."
— Revelation 3:20a

I found Clarence Larkin's commentary on this passage most eye-opening.

> These words are generally quoted as an appeal to sinners, but they are not, they are addressed to a Church, and to a Church in whose midst Christ once stood, but now found Himself excluded and standing outside knocking for admittance. This is the most startling thing recorded in the New Testament, that it is possible for a church to be outwardly prosperous and yet have no Christ in its midst, and be unconscious of the fact. This is a description of a Christless Church.
>
> Oh the EXCLUDED CHRIST. Excluded from His own nation, for they Rejected Him; excluded from the world, for it Crucified Him; excluded from His Church, for He stands outside its door

> Knocking for Entrance. How did Christ come to be outside the Church? He had been within it once or there never would have been a Church. How did He come to leave? It is clear that they had not thrust Him out, for they do not seem to have missed His presence. They continued to worship Him, to sing His praises, and engage in all manner of Christian service, yet He had withdrawn. Why? The reason is summed up in one word—Worldliness.

I have always been one to pursue truth. From the moment I started a personal journey with Christ, I wanted to know Him. I joined and faithfully attended regular Bible studies while also studying independently on my own. I developed an insatiable appetite for reading and read every kind of Christian book I could get my hands on. I poured through my huge concordance, took classes, and went to conferences. I asked countless questions and observed every atmosphere I found myself in, so that I could learn and grow. I wanted to understand this "body of Christ" I was now part of and where I fit in it.

I was hungry, but spiritually, I didn't know the difference between eating on husks and real food. When the prodigal son was hungry, he fed off the husks, but when he was starving, he turned to his father! I was hungry in my early years trying to satisfy my growing appetite by feeding off husks, but in the journey of surrender, I found myself starving. Rather than feed off anything else, I, too, turned to my Father. When He knocked me to my knees, He made me crave Him even more.

Though I may have come across rather harsh in my evaluation of today's state of the Church, I acknowledge that there are many churches and church leaders that are faithful at running the hard race on behalf of their flocks. However, I do grieve over many churches because, as so eloquently stated by Clarence Larkin, I believe they've lost the presence of their Lord and they don't even realize it. I continue to interact with many people and organizations within the body of Christ, but my heart aches watching how we have settled for mere morsels of Him when He desires to fill us to a fullness few of us have experienced.

The Church needs to stop feeding off the husks of others and learn how to starve for our Father. We may not want to hear this today, but I believe we are the Church of Laodicea mentioned in Revelation 3. We are neither hot nor cold; we are tepid. Christ would rather have us frozen or boiling, but right now we are lukewarm. We have an absence of "spiritual heat" and "scriptural meat." We boast of our influence on the world while Christ sees our poverty of heart.

I used to greet people as they were arriving to church and thank them for coming as they were leaving. Rarely did anyone walk out of the door glorifying God nor were they so overcome by His presence that they could barely speak or even make eye contact because the weight of His glory was so powerfully resting on them. No, rather it was always about what a wonderful sermon so and so gave, as they giggled about the funny stories or witty delivery. It's no wonder the Holy Spirit bid me "to come die."

The Holy Spirit is the One who does God's bidding. He's the One sent to live inside of you and me and empower us to be overcomers. He's the One who humbles you, cries through you, feeds you, sustains you, helps you endure, and gives you joy. We preach, for example, on tithing as if money will evangelize the world, when the very One sent to evangelize the world is conveniently left out. He's the One that *"looses the loins of kings"* and commands the gates to be opened (Isaiah 45:1, NASB). We can have all the money in the world, but unless God opens the doors to where He wants it deposited, we labor in vain.

He goes before us to make crooked places straight, breaking to pieces gates of bronze and cutting bars of iron (Isaiah 45:2). Meaning, nothing is too hard for Him. Yet, in only but a relatively few churches is the Holy Spirit given His rightful place. Outwardly, we're dressed to the nines, even our churches. They look like trendy coffee shops, roadhouse bars, and musical theaters. They're adorned in some of the finest materials, but God counsels us to purchase Christ. *"I counsel you to buy from Me gold refined in the fire, that you may be rich; and white garments, that you may be clothed, that the same of your nakedness may not be revealed..."* (Revelation 3:18). The Laodiceans were famous for making raven black woolen garments, but Jesus was challenging them to exchange them for His white garments. Many of our churches are famous, but they're dressed in black wool.

My desire for you is to have Christ stop knocking at the door of your heart, and for you to give Him His rightful place on the throne of it. The Bible says that while men slept, the enemy sowed tares among the wheat (Matthew 13:24-30). What is the enemy sowing while we're sleeping? We're urged to get up early to go to school and work or to catch a plane, but how often are we urged to get up before school or work to pray? Too often, a woman who fills up her day with golf, tennis, workouts, day spas, and lunch outings is considered well-rounded and socially accepted, but a woman giving the same hours to prayer is talked about as being religiously off-balanced and dangerously radical. Our whole sense of value must be revolutionized!

We must develop a spiritual appetite. If we do, learning to hunger and thirst after Him, we are promised to not only dine with Him but are also granted a place to sit at His throne. But if we do not, and we stay where we're at—being tepid (and socially "acceptable")—He will spew us out of His mouth. Careful, Church, if we say that we are rich, we are instead like the Laodiceans: *"wretched, miserable, poor, blind, and naked,"* (Revelation 3:17).

Reflect and Respond

- Where is God in your church? Is He knocking outside to be let in? If He is let in, who or what commands the time, the Holy Spirit and His leading or the program in place?
- In Africa, the women danced and praised God loudly and in utter abandon. They giggled when they saw how we tried to dance with them. How do you view Pentecostals, Catholics, home churches, Charismatics, Non-Denominational churches, (list others)? Do they make you uncomfortable in any way? Describe.
- How does this impact how you see worship in heaven with every tribe and tongue?

Real Pentecost Results

We have underestimated the needs for our day. What is it going to take to realize that we need a baptism of fire? We need another Pentecost. When those first-century disciples, which included women, were told to go to Jerusalem and wait for the power Jesus said would come (Acts 1:8), they went. They not only waited; they *"continued with one accord in prayer and supplication"* (Acts 1:14). How long did they do that? Pentecost (named so in Greek) was an annual feast day that the Jews celebrated, which was always 50 days after Passover (Leviticus 23:15). After His death on Passover, Jesus appeared to His disciples several times over a period of 40 days (Acts 1:3), so they waited 10 days from His ascension until Pentecost.

How does one stay focused in prayer for that long? Most likely, they were gripped by a growing hunger for what was to come, thirsting with anticipation for the power Jesus had promised. When was the last time you went through a prayer time like that? We need to be gripped by a cry for revival to come. It *will* come…at a cost. Don't think for a moment God doesn't want this to happen. He does. But it will come to a Church that is humbled before Him, gathering together in prayer as "one." He cannot pour out His fire on His Church until we learn what it requires to carry His fire. He's an all-consuming fire, which means you must be empty to be consumed by Him.

Pentecost meant power, but it also meant prison. It meant enduement, but it also meant banishment. It meant favor with God, but it also brought hatred from men. Pentecost brought great miracles, but it also brought many obstacles. The Holy Spirit turns the world upside down but leaves His fruit along the way, and Jesus said the world will know us by our fruit. The world will know us when we are one. A fire is self-announcing, but before the fire fills our hearts, our hearts need to be cleansed of sin. What God has cleansed, He fills, and whom God fills, He uses.

The life of a Christian is one of battle. That's why we need to be fueled properly. Hungering and thirsting after righteousness means we go into the battle with the battle plans of heaven. We are filled with the will of God being delivered through us. It's not an easy road. We are called to a life of holy living if we are truly wanting to look like our Savior. Attacks on the early church from the outside were easily detected. But today's Church needs the gift of discernment from the Holy Spirit to detect subtle efforts to destroy it from within. Wolves have come in wearing sheep's clothing, which means the wolves look, talk, walk, and appear like a Christian…but they're deceiving many.

God is kind, merciful, and loving, but He's also not afraid to pronounce His judgment upon sinfulness as recorded in Acts 5. Ananias and his wife Sapphira sold their farm and planned to hold back some of the proceeds to keep for themselves, rather than share the wealth among the early church, which was customary. God revealed this to Peter, who confronted Ananias first. When Ananias heard Peter's God-revealed accusation, that Ananias lied about the money, he fell over dead. No sooner had his body been removed than his wife entered the room. Peter encountered the wife and gave her a chance to come clean, but she lied. In that moment, she, too, dropped dead. They were not just lying to Peter; they were lying to God's representative, which means they were lying to God. If a Spirit-filled couple living next to the cauldron of heat, known as the early Church, could face such a fate, we have to wonder what is going to happen to us? What is staying God's hand today?'

Somehow, over the centuries, we have done what would have been unheard of in the early church—make Christ appear dull. On the Acts 2 day of Pentecost, the world thought men were drunk with "new wine." Maybe it takes such "drunk" men to ignore the world and ignite the Church! I don't know. But what I do know is that God said when judgment comes, it begins in the house of God first. That statement alone sends me straight to the throne of grace seeking mercy. Friends, it is so important that we get right with God. It's time to get hungry and thirsty. We spend more time planning how hungry we'll be when we get to the Thanksgiving Day table than how we should feel daily in our relationship with Jesus Christ. I don't know about you, but I wake up hungry for Him. I can no longer go to places where I'm fed a granola bar portion of Jesus Christ. I need the meat of His Word, the fullness of His Spirit, and the refreshment of true fellowship.

The Wrestling of Jacob

It's critical we learn to follow the gospel of the Kingdom of God. When we become poor in spirit, we begin to mourn and break. God is looking for a man or woman like that. When He see that you are humble with a contrite spirit, He knows He can do something with you. We must come to a point where we mourn our ineffectiveness on the earth, and hunger and thirst for what is real. It's a blessed thing to get to the state of hungering and thirsting after righteousness because we can then better discern if something is God's voice, not man's. As a result, we can be led by the true Shepherd, Jesus Christ. When we hunger and thirst, God's grief has finally reached our hearts. Now, He can fill us, so we can take the message of the gospel to the ends of the earth.

Have you ever hungered and thirsted after righteousness? Have you ever gotten so serious that you seek God with all your heart, soul, and might and nothing would keep you from Him until you find Him? If we do that, He says we shall be "filled," meaning we shall be satisfied. Imagine a time in your life when you felt so hungry or so thirsty that all you could think about was getting something in your stomach or drinking a cool glass of water. When we get to that degree of hunger and thirst, it's difficult to think of anything else except being filled by the very thing we crave. Once we eat our food and enjoy our cool glass of water, we are satisfied. We can relax and continue with whatever else it is we were planning on doing that day.

That is how it is with Christ. It is possible to become so hungry and thirsty for Him that we can scarcely think of anything else until we have our fill of Him. Be careful here though. We are to hunger and thirst *after righteousness*, which means we will never be satisfied until God makes us…righteous! God has put Himself under a holy obligation to fulfill this. He must follow through with those who are hungering and thirsting after Him, those who are willing to lay aside everything in life and get desperate with Him! When we do that, He will make us righteous. He will not turn His face away from you when you're seeking Him. *"And you will seek Me and find Me, when you search for Me with all your heart"* (Jeremiah 29:13). When have you done that? When have you laid it all down? Oh, Lord, give us something real rather than a life of carnality and lies.

There are two kinds of righteousness spoken of in the Bible: righteousness imputed and righteousness imparted. Righteousness imputed is God declaring you righteous through faith in His Son Jesus Christ. You are justified (found acceptable to God) because your *faith alone* has been *accounted* to you *as* righteousness. But the righteousness in the Beatitudes is "to conform" or have His nature imparted to us. It's also called sanctification. This is a righteousness given *as a result of* your hungering and thirsting. It won't be given automatically; you must seek it out.

We must seek Christ with holy desperation and wrestle with Him over it like Jacob wrestled with God during the night. When he sensed God withdrawing from him, Jacob refused to be released without God blessing him first. "You've wrestled too long, child. I must let you go," God tells him. Jacob responds, *"I will not let You go unless You bless me"* (Genesis 32:26)! Have you ever said that to God? Have you ever been in that place where you can't bear living your life without having God's best first?

God's nature had to get imparted to Jacob because God was changing Jacob's identity in that moment. It's no different than what He's changing in you. He wants His new nature to rise up and take hold of you. He wants your new identity in Him to be the result of this wrestling you've been going through in dying to self, mourning, and learning to live a life of surrender and meekness. Do you see what He's doing? He's giving you a new name, a new life, and a new identity through His Son Jesus Christ. After that wrestling match, Jacob was no longer Jacob but Israel, which means "prince with God." Jacob became a prince of God not of man. In the spiritual realm, he was the greatest man on earth at that time. God made Him righteous. Who will you emerge as when God fills you? When will you get desperate enough to find out?

If a man stays in the desert for days and days, he will get desperately hungry and thirsty. You can write him a million-dollar check, and it won't mean a thing to him because you are not giving him what he's hungering or thirsting for. The same is true for us. If we are thirsting for righteousness, we won't stop seeking God until He makes us righteous. *"Be holy, for I am Holy"* should always be echoing in our spirit. As a result of absolute surrender, like Jacob, God takes control and fills us with His fullness through His Spirit.

The Holy Spirit is a person, and to be filled by Him is to be controlled by Him. When you absolutely surrender to God, when He takes control and your fight is given up, He emerges. The only way to change our lukewarm state is to surrender, wrestle with God, and let the Holy Spirit take over. Far too long we have pushed the Holy Spirit to the sidelines and grieved Him. We've quenched the very Helper sent for us. There's only one way to get the Church hot again—through the person of the Holy Spirit.

Reflect and Respond

- When have you searched for God with *all* your heart…*all* of it? Tell God what that time looked like. Maybe it's now.
- What is it going to take for you to get desperate for God? Describe.
- What do you think of the person of the Holy Spirit? What have you been taught about Him? To be filled by Him is to be controlled by Him. Are you controlled by Him? What does it mean to you to be controlled by Him?

An Acceptable Offering

"Blessed are those who hunger and thirst for righteousness, for they shall be filled" (Matthew 5:6). What a statement! It's a "good" negative before a positive again. We must learn to hunger before we can be filled. We're such a "now" generation of people that we want to be filled with minimal time or effort. The Lord must become the object of our love. That is why this beatitude comes after dying to self and grieving over sin; it is an act of selflessness. Emptying ourselves makes us hungry. And what happens after we eat? We are full. That is the blessing that comes after we hunger for holiness; He fills us and satisfies us. It's a promise from Scripture—we will be given what we desire!

In the story of Cain and Abel, God was pleased with the sacrifice of the firstborn of the flock that Abel offered but did not look favorably on Cain's offering of the fruit of the ground. Cain was discouraged, and in his discouragement, God gave him a warning: *"If you do well, will you not be accepted? And if you do not do well, sin lies at the door. And its desire is for you, but you should rule over it"* (Genesis 4:7). Sin desires you and me! It will always tell us to stop short from giving God our first fruits every day. What I mean is we come up with every excuse on why we have little time for Him.

We are too busy to pray, too busy to do our Bible study, too busy attending sports events to attend church, or too busy to have time to serve, or fill in the blank. We are filled with reasons for why we can't keep appointments with God; yet, we rearrange our schedules, find sitters, or skip other events to attend the things that are important to us. We have to ask: Is what we offer of ourselves to God each day any different than what Cain offered? Are we giving an "acceptable" sacrifice of ourselves to Him each day or are we giving ourselves to someone or something else?

It's time to get desperate. How many more people do we have to watch die, become addicted, lose faith and turn from God on our watch? It's time to bear fruit, the fruit of righteousness. It's time to make room for Him. When we're empty, He pours in, fills up, and satisfies. That is why the Beatitudes are crucial. That is why Jesus started the Sermon on the Mount with them. A day is coming when all who are in Christ and belong to Him shall stand in the presence of God faultless, blameless, and without spot and wrinkle. All blemishes will be gone. We will be made perfect. This is what He is making us ready for. This is what He wants us to hunger for, so that *"When Christ who is our life appears, you also will appear with Him in glory"* (Colossians 3:4).

Church of Laodicea, it's time to let our Lord back into the church. The worldliness that has consumed it has blinded us and caused us to be poor, miserable, and naked. Jesus never wanted us to get spoon fed every week. He wants us to seek His Kingdom so He can add "all" things unto us (Matthew 6:33). It's time, Church, to seek His Kingdom and do things His way again, but His way is being diluted with and overcome by the world. It's time to come out of the world and be separate. He stands, ever patiently at the door, and knocks. Do you hear Him? How did He ever get on the outside of the door to begin with, and how did we not notice?

Tune your ears to His Spirit and be a voice of one that cries in the wilderness "prepare the way for the Lord." He wants to be let back in to the Church. He wants to take us by the hand and lead us down the narrow path. He beckons you, "Follow Me."

"Blessed are those who hunger and thirst after righteousness, for they shall be filled."

PRACTICAL PRACTICES

CHAPTER 5

Church

Write your findings in a journal or notepad.

Come 15 minutes early to church this week and try to stay 15 minutes after. Use the time to pray for your church, its pastors and leaders, the musicians, and other ministries. Thank Him for your church.

Home

In your prayer times this week focus on exalting who God is. Read Psalms 145-149 out loud.

Practice hungering and thirsting after righteousness by consecrating a "fast" unto God this week. God says "*when* you pray" and "*when* you fast," meaning He expects us to do both. Fasting is a supernatural act of God that basically cleans out our pipes so that He can flow freely through them. It's an act of obedience and love. During your fast, try to redirect your thoughts from being hungry to being hungry for God, or from being thirsty to being thirsty for Him. Use those times you are hungry and thirsty to worship, pray, or read your Scriptures. Try one of two fasts:

- Fast for half a day by denying yourself breakfast, coffee, and a mid-morning snack.
- Fast for 24 hours by not eating after dinner, during the night, in the morning and lunch. Then resume eating again at the next dinner. Half of that time, you are asleep, so it's an easy way to try a 24-hour fast.

Read

Meditate on these verses:

- Read John 6:32-40.
- Read 1 John 3:1-24.
- Read Isaiah 45:8.
- Read Jeremiah 23:1-8.
- James 1:12-20.

Listen

- "One Thirst" by Steffany Frizzell & Jeremy Riddle, *Bethel Live: Be Lifted High*
- "My Soul Longs" by Grace Williams, *Overflow*
- "As the Deer" by Matt Gilman, *Awaken Love*
- "Closer" by Steffany Frizzell-Gretzinger, *Bethel Live, For the Sake of the World*

CHAPTER 6

Blessed Are the Merciful

"Show mercy and compassion for others, just as your heavenly Father overflows with mercy and compassion for all. Jesus said, 'Forsake the habit of criticizing and judging others, and then you will not be criticized and judged in return. Don't look at others and pronounce them guilty, and you will not experience guilty accusations yourself. Forgive over and over and you will be forgiven over and over."

— Luke 6:36-37, TPT

It was date night! My husband and I, along with another couple in town, had plans to get together. We decided to do something different and thought a sunset hike would be just the thing on this beautiful evening. We brought our two golden retrievers, and they brought their lab, and away we went into the meadow that led to a hike that took us to Bergen Peak. Our friends rarely take the "road more traveled," and as such, we did not take a path to get there, but rather cut our own path through the trees as we kept climbing higher. I was no way near the kind of physical shape my husband and our friends were in, so you can imagine that if they found themselves breathing hard, I was really struggling!

We stopped on occasion to catch our breath and even at one point had to stop as a huge herd of elk came barreling up the mountain side in front of us, running with incredible ease as they disappeared through the thick trees. We almost lost one of our dogs in the herd as he tried to chase them down. It was an incredible sight to behold. Had we taken a different route, we would have never witnessed that moment. We finally arrived at the peak or close enough to it, right when the sun was starting its descent for the day. We found some huge rocks to perch ourselves on and took in the view around us.

Our friend took off his backpack and proceeded to unpack a little surprise. He had an array of cheeses, meats, and other goodies we could snack on as we watched the sun set. It was the best meat and cheese I've ever had! After pouring out the energy it took to reach the top, it was so refreshing to be filled back up before descending back down towards home. We savored every bite! I still think about that date night and chalk it up as one of my favorites because it reminded me of the importance of changing things up in our lives. Dates don't always have to look a certain way, nor does our walk with God. Sometimes we have to get off the main path, or the wide path, to see the beauty in a path less traveled. Although more difficult, it yields a more satisfying result.

This is also true of the Beatitudes. We are learning that Christianity is all about taking a very narrow road that prepares us for God's Kingdom living. Christianity is about character, not about "trying to be Christians." Many of us have fallen into a pattern of doing the same thing in our Christian walk day in and day out following the same well-worn path. Should we be really honest with ourselves, we may be starting to find our walk with Christ dull.

However, the narrow path offers us the opportunity to realize that it's not dull at all; in fact, it's like climbing a mountain. The first three spiritual laws, or beatitudes, are similar to climbing the first part of the mountain. Becoming poor in spirit, grieving sin, and understanding meekness emphasize the vital importance of a deep awareness of our need for Him. We are pouring out what we're made of to reach a destination. We reach the summit with the fourth spiritual law, hungering and thirsting for Him. Then comes God's provision for that need; He fills us. We see the result of being filled as we begin our descent down. We become merciful. *"Blessed are the merciful, for they shall obtain mercy"* (Matthew 5:7).

It is only when we are filled that we can now start working on the rest of our journey, one in which we experience God's incredible mercy. However, we must be careful not to miss that already up to this point, our Lord has been giving us signs and evidence of the work of His grace in our souls. The "merciful" in this text have already been experiencing an incredible amount of His mercy on this journey of the narrow path. The promise was already given to us in part when we received a renewed heart.

It's merciful of our Lord to lead us down a path of being emptied of our pride and brought to see how undeserving we are in the sight of God. These last few weeks, we have been made to feel our own weakness. We have been looking at the true condition of our hearts, mourning over past sins that have alienated us from Christ, and recognizing our ingratitude and rebellion towards Him and His Holy Spirit. Because of God's incredible mercy, we have been weaned from the world, filled up on the fullness of His Spirit, and are now ready to release that grace by being merciful to others. This narrow path is definitely a road less traveled by the world.

A Christian is "something" before he does "anything." Our Lord is taking this vessel He made, you and me, and is searching it, testing it, and subjecting it to thoughts, people, and experiences to make sure the inside of the vessel is clean enough to pour His substance into. No one wants to pour something out of a dirty pitcher, especially if it's being poured out to serve others. That is exactly what you are—a vessel, cleaned out, filled up, and ready to be poured out. Being merciful to others is not an outgrowth of our own doing but another gift of His grace towards us, another fruit you are bearing for the Kingdom of God. You see beloved, He has already been working out His mercy in you throughout the journey thus far. His promise is that the merciful shall be filled. Was not His mercy towards us to the full?

Many of us are trying so hard to "be" Christ-like that we fail to realize we must possess a certain character in order to be a certain kind of person, in this case, a Christian. *Our* emphasis is on doing rather than on being, which is a false gospel. Please don't miss the importance of that last sentence. The *gospel* puts a greater weight on our attitude than upon our actions. When Christians are under persecution, it's not because of anything they did but because of who they are. Now they may be persecuted in the middle of an action, but the root of the persecution is because of their belief.

We are not meant to control our Christianity; it is meant to control us. We think that because Scripture says *"take up your cross and follow Me"* that it means we are immediately put into action. No. We need to live His truth first that says, *"it is no longer I who live, but Christ lives in me"* (Galatians 2:20). A cross is a heavy thing to carry, and following Jesus is incredibly difficult, but God knows what He's doing. He knows what He asks of us. He knows what it's going to take to bear His image. The merciful in this beatitude are those who have already obtained mercy, the mercy God has given them to be able to walk this path to begin with. It should be inevitable now for you to display and extend mercy to others because of what has been done for you.

Reflect and Respond

- Is it difficult for you to just "be" with God or do you feel like you need to be "doing" something for Him?
- Do you feel God's mercy upon you on this journey? Does having His mercy at work towards you make you more merciful to others?

Slaves to Love

We are not merciful because we are naturally tenderhearted; we are merciful because God has made us poor in spirit. We are not merciful because of generous families and family heritage; we are merciful because we mourned and were comforted. We are not merciful because we sought the esteem of our fellow man, but because we ourselves were meek and lowly, inheriting the earth. We felt the hunger and the thirst and are merciful because we only hope that others in the world will begin the same powerful journey that will bend their hearts to conform to the Savior.

Jesus modeled the Sermon on the Mount when He first emptied Himself coming to earth as a man: *"but emptied himself, taking the form of a servant, being made in the likeness of men"* (Philippians 2:7, ASV). The word "servant" in this verse is actually "bondman or slave." Jesus emptied Himself to come as a slave, whose position is even lower than a servant. Paul, James, and Peter recognized the importance of this lower position as they introduce themselves in their epistles as bondservants, or slaves, to Christ. In order to truly understand how to extend mercy, they made themselves slaves to Christ, or, in other words, slaves to love. This is how we must learn to approach each and every situation and person we encounter—as a bondservant of Christ, serving them in love.

The spiritual laws of God's Kingdom are in such contradiction to our own earthly laws. The early Church understood this and as a result spent much of their time in making decisions through prayer and fasting, sacrificially serving God and others through both practices. Both require something from us spiritually and physically, yielding an abundance of spiritual fruit, one being mercy. Generally, prayer and fasting are done very little in the Church today, let alone in our private lives. Yet, they are the two examples, we're told in Scriptures, that grow our authority.

> Then one of the crowd answered and said, "Teacher, I brought You my son, who has a mute spirit. And wherever it seizes him, it throws him down; he foams at the mouth, gnashes his teeth, and becomes rigid. So I spoke to Your disciples, that they should cast it out, but they could not." He answered him and said, "O faithless generation, how long shall I be with you? How long shall I bear with you? Bring him to Me."
>
> Then they brought him to Him. And when he saw Him, immediately the spirit convulsed him, and he fell on the ground and wallowed, foaming at the mouth. So He asked his father, "How long has this been happening to him?" And he said, "From childhood. And often he has thrown him both into the fire and into the water to destroy him. But if You can do anything, have compassion on us and help us."
>
> Jesus said to him, "If you can believe, all things are possible to him who believes." Immediately the father of the child cried out and said with tears, "Lord, I believe; help my unbelief!" When Jesus saw that the people came running together, He rebuked the unclean spirit, saying to it: "Deaf and dumb spirit,

> I command you, come out of him and enter him no more!" Then the spirit cried out, convulsed him greatly, and came out of him. And he became as one dead, so that many said, "He is dead."
>
> But Jesus took him by the hand and lifted him up, and he arose. And when He had come into the house, His disciples asked Him privately, "Why could we not cast it out?" So He said to them, *"This kind can come out by nothing but prayer and fasting"* (Mark 9:17-29).

Mercy desired to see this son set free from demonic oppression as the man asked for Jesus to have "compassion," which is another word for mercy. A merciful heart is needed to minister to a lost and hurting world. Mercy is our engine; it's what motivates us to act. However, we also need to have an established life of prayer and fasting to walk in the authority of Christ. All of it comes from a place of surrender and an outworking of His grace towards us. If the devil knows prayer and fasting grows our authority, and that we can use our authority to cast out demons, he know it really causes problems for his kingdom. This is exactly why he will do everything in his power to keep you off of the narrow path. A yielded heart is a heart that is a slave to Christ, filled with the mercy of God. That only comes from a place of prayer and intimacy with Him.

Why did I include this important point with the topic on mercy? Because we are watching a world set itself on fire, and many of us do not know how to respond. We are watching addictions skyrocket, evil increase, and mental illness manifest in violent ways; yet, we have no idea how to pray or act, and so we feel helpless. At this point in our journey, we can look upon these things with mercy first and respond according to God's ways, through prayer and fasting, which will produce a result we never thought possible. Mercy is what drives us to pray and fast, which causes strongholds to be pulled down and the salt in us to start doing what's it's designed to do—prevent decay. So being merciful is a powerful yet subtle attribute of God's nature that He is developing in you. Don't minimize its importance.

The Goodness of God

Being merciful bears another attribute of God—His kindness and goodness towards the world, especially towards those who are suffering. The poor and suffering rock His heart, as modeled by Jesus. He could not see someone in need and pass him by. No merciful man can forget the poor. With Christ's nature emerging in us, it's impossible to shut off our flow of compassion to such a person. The truly merciful are considerate, thinking of the poor often, especially when surrounded by comforts of their own. On cold, rainy, windy, snowy evenings in the dark of night, the merciful are wondering how the poor are getting by in their year-old socks, scantily clad clothes, and shared bedding, most likely sleeping on the streets somewhere. They must do something about it or they cannot rest.

One night, a group of us went to a church in the city to serve the poor and set up stations to wash and anoint feet. When their turn was over, we completed it with a fresh pair of socks. Their faces said it all. They took in the moment in quiet humility followed with genuine thankfulness. Many cried…we cried! It was a quiet ride home as our own hearts were cut to the core reflecting on what exactly brought these precious people to this lot in life. I came home, crawled into my warm bed, and knew something had shifted within me. Where God has given a new heart and new spirit, there is great tenderness towards the poor and to people in general. All saints, all believers in Christ Jesus, are pictures of Christ Himself, but a poor saint is a picture of Christ set in the same frame in which Christ's picture must be set, the frame of humble poverty.

Reflect and Respond

- Picture yourself in the inner city near where you live. What comes through your mind when you drive past the tent camps, drunkenness, and drug-induced stupor? Be honest. Do you see them as lazy or dirty? Are you secretly happy that's not you?
- How often do you serve the poor, other than holidays?
- Do you believe in the enemy, Satan? Or hell? Explain.
- Do you believe people can have demons? Do you believe demons can be cast out like Jesus did in the story in Mark?
- When you reflect on your journey so far, do you feel as though your authority in God is growing? Explain.

Outside the Camp

We don't just believe in Jesus in order to be saved from hell; we believe upon Jesus because He's a friend of sinners and died showing us that. This is exactly why Jesus had to suffer "outside the camp" or "outside the gate" when He was put to death on the cross. *"For the high priest carries the blood of animals into the holiest chamber as a sacrifice for sin, and then burns the bodies of the animals outside the city. And Jesus, our sin-sacrifice, also suffered death outside the city walls to make us holy by his own blood. So we must arise and join him outside the religious "walls" and bear his disgrace"* (Hebrews 13:11-13, TPT).

This was in fulfillment of Old Testament law when the High Priest burned the sin offering "outside the camp" (Exodus 29:14). It was such a disgrace to God that He required the offering not to be burnt upon the altar where other sacrifices took place but to take it "outside the camp." In other words, God despised sin so much that the animal that was slaughtered for a person's sin had to be removed from the camp altogether so that it would not only be removed from His people, but from God Himself. He did not want sin anywhere near His dwelling place.

During Moses' day, the great camp of Israel was carefully designed so that the tents were placed in order by tribes. Each tribe had a specifically assigned place so that all twelve of them surrounded the tabernacle of the Lord, which was in the center of the camp. There were also a few little huts a little further off outside the camp reserved for anyone considered "unclean." These were not permitted to go to the sanctuary to present their offerings, so they had to live outside the camp from everyone else because they were either lepers or had been made unclean for some other reason (Numbers 5:2).

This was true for lepers during the time of Jesus also, as they would have to cry out, "Unclean, unclean, unclean," as people came near them. They were announcing their state so as not to infect others with the disease. These poor, destitute, diseased people were sent to live "outside the gate" so as not to pass their disease on to others in Jerusalem. To be outside the gate was considered a disgrace to Jews of Jesus time.

These lepers are a "type" of you and me in our natural state without Christ. In our unsaved state, we are considered "unclean" and outside the gate of heaven. Maybe it's someone who is poor and filled with shame, or a prostitute who so disregards herself that she feels unworthy of saving, or the criminal whose guilt is suffocating him as he wonders how he got to such a place in life that he would have to steal other people's belongings to get by. We do not know the stories yet, but we know there are many.

That's why Christ is the fulfillment of Scriptures. He knows who lives outside the camp, and He is merciful to them still. He Himself can relate to lepers, the poor, and the prostitutes because He, too, was sent outside the camp to die. He died with the unclean and then washed them in His blood of mercy and saved every last one of them that would hope in His mercy and in His name. In every way, He has identified with us and met our needs. That is why He imparted His merciful heart to ours. He wants us, too, to go outside the camp to the unclean, poor, and unloved people of the world and share in their sufferings as He did. We can still wash Christ's feet by caring for the poorest of His people.

An Eye for Those Who Mourn

Having a merciful heart for the poor is as important as having a merciful heart for those with a sad countenance or those who struggle with depression. The merciful heart has an eye for those who are mourning and filled with such a sad state that they seldom have one bright day in the whole year. And even though some of these souls are people who are of excellent spirit and character and love the Lord their God with everything in them, they are subject to a bondage few can truly understand apart from mercy.

Many of us ignore the realities of depression and sadness and chalk it up to other things, hoping the person will just take some medicine and be over it. As a result, we tend to steer clear of such people hoping we won't get sucked into such a state. Although we may not fully understand the cause, to them, the pain is very real. Rather than analyze it and come up with solutions for it, with God's mercy, we love them in the midst of it. That is where, as merciful people, we pull from divine Scriptures words of comfort because there is only One who can comfort them—the Comforter Himself, the Holy Spirit.

Scriptures always remind us about who God is. Jesus our Lord sought after the wounded; He bound up the broken hearted, and He healed the sick. In His mercy, He gently reminds us that we are to be imitators of Him, showing the greatest interest to those who are in the saddest place of life. If we are hard-hearted in any way, we are not what we ought to be. When we are in our right state, we are tender, full of compassion, and merciful because we have received these things first hand as we have been learning from the Lord Jesus. As a result, we, the merciful, are blessed, but there may be a time in the future when we will obtain mercy from others when we need it. Perhaps one of us will experience a season of depression or sadness or find ourselves on the streets hungry and thirsty. We have the promise and assurance from our Lord that we will obtain mercy.

This brings me to a very important point on our journey, the topic of forgiveness. As people who are filled with the mercy of God, may we never take to heart the offenses done towards us or the insults thrown our way, intentionally or unintentionally. Although many of us have experienced these things, with cuts almost too deep to heal, bear in mind that if we want to be forgiven, we must choose to forgive others, regardless of what they have done to us. This can be a painstaking process for some. There are injuries to our bodies, souls, spirits, minds, and emotions that run very deep for many of us, but as children of God, we realize that we are not perfect and that we live with imperfect people. Those who wounded us are also wounded, and they, too, will need the mercy of God as much as we will. Let us pray for our accusers, our abusers, and our enemies.

Reflect and Respond

- Is there anyone you have not forgiven on this journey? Ask the Holy Spirit to search your heart now.
- Who do you know that struggles with depression, sadness, or a sense of worthlessness?
- Ask the Holy Spirit to show you how best to minister mercy to them this week?

Who are we to judge?

Lastly, may we be of such a merciful heart as to have mercy for the outwardly sinful person. This is going to be a very challenging for Christians who have not been walking this narrow path of holiness where we are truly crucified with Him. We must remember from how far we've fallen and how Christ went outside the camp to pick us up. Paul tells us, *"Therefore put to death your members which are on the earth: fornication, uncleanness, passion, evil desire, and covetousness, which is idolatry. Because of these things the wrath of God is coming upon the sons of disobedience, in which you yourselves once walked when you lived in them"* (Colossians 3:5-7).

We too once walked as the world and were sons of disobedience. Because we have obtained mercy and our Lord has led us down this narrow path, may we always remember those who are still walking through the wide gate of destruction and never think too highly of ourselves to not want to help them. This is where we have to be very careful of hypocrisy. There are many men and women who are living in vile sin and know they are; yet, they go into society and are received as if they are the most respectable persons in the world. This is true of both believers and unbelievers. They speak of virtue but accuse others of having no virtue while they are indulging in hidden vices. This is why we must never, ever put any person on a pedestal of any kind, believer or unbeliever. We have to be able to discern the gravity of their sin and how much God detests it but always think kindly of the sinner.

The merciful Christian does not shut anyone out. In fact, the lower we have to go to reach or befriend a person, the greater our honor. Jesus was filled with mercy. He saw people as sheep without a shepherd and was moved with compassion and caused Him to walk in the miraculous. Mercy paved the way as He preached with authority, cast out demons, and healed the sick, lame, deaf, and mute. *"But as for me, I will come into Your house in the multitude of Your mercy; in fear of You I will worship toward Your holy temple"* (Psalm 5:7). Mercy and justice are the foundation of God's throne and were the foundation of Christ's ministry on the earth. Mercy is in abundance in our Father's house, but reverence for it is required. Moving in any way on behalf of God's Kingdom requires a fear of the Lord and incredible mercy.

After hungering and thirsting for righteousness, we find we are filled with mercy. Our attitude towards everybody else must be completely and entirely changed. We can no longer look upon people as we used to. While grace looks down upon sin as a whole, mercy looks especially upon its miserable consequences. The Lord is teaching us how to look upon people with a merciful heart and desire to relieve their suffering and wants that to be part of our world view.

What do we have that we did not receive first? God looked down upon man and was moved with mercy to pour out His grace upon us. *"For who makes you differ from another? And what do you have that you did not receive"* (1 Corinthians 4:7a)? We were recipients of God's mercy and when we are filled with Him, no less is expected of us to give to others. Jesus is telling us to treat others as we have been treated by God. We have been treated with incredible mercy, so we need to treat others with the same.

Jesus came to seek and save what was lost. I look upon the world and deeply grieve over how far it keeps falling. In that place of grief and then God's infilling, I find myself never satisfied leaving people where I find them. Whether they work at the grocery store or gas station or they're my neighbor, I don't hesitate to tell them about what God can do for them. When the hand on the man in the deli department is shaking, I feel mercy. I tell him that I serve a God that heals hands and ask if I could please pray for his hand. When a young man asks for money to fill up his tank at gas station on his way to a drug-fueled concert, I am filled with mercy. I pump the gas in his red gas container, sharing with him how much God loves him and how He wants to put His call on his life. People are incredible touched by God's mercy. They feel remembered and, whether they say it or not, they feel loved.

It's mercy that causes many of us to fill the "watches of the night" with prayer rotations so that while people sleep and the atmosphere is quiet, prayers can ascend unhindered to the throne room of heaven. Mercy is where it all begins. We must ask our Father to birth His heart in us for others. If we are debtors to Christ and understand the mercy bestowed on us, there should be no pride left in us to hold it back towards others.

This is why Christ, as the Sanctifier, must be permitted to work out His will in us and turn us into His image. Sanctification is the work of the Spirit of God within us to transform us. *"But we all, with unveiled face, beholding as in a mirror the glory of the Lord, are being transformed into the same image from glory to glory, just as by the Spirit of the Lord"* (2 Corinthians 3:18).

Are you merciful? Are you sorry for every sinner even though that sinner offends you? Do you look at the world and see how so many have been duped by Satan? Does it cause you to want to move in compassion? That is our test. Again, it reminds me of the trail we blazed on our date night hike. We would have missed the glorious splendor of what awaited us had we chosen a different path, the path that everyone took. Keep walking this narrow path. Glory awaits.

"Blessed is the merciful, for that shall obtain mercy."

PRACTICAL PRACTICES

CHAPTER 6

Church

Write your findings in a journal or notepad.

Explain how you know your church or congregation is a place of mercy.

Find a way that your church is serving the poor or downtrodden. Ask for information and then pray and ask God if you should sign up and help. This may go along with #2 under "Home."

Look around at church over the next month and ask God to show you someone who is in need of mercy. Befriend them.

Home

Think of someone "outside the gate" you can invite to church, maybe someone you do not know very well. Invite them. Do not be disappointed if they say no and invite them again at a later date. They'll be secretly touched you asked.

Find an organization near you where you can start regularly serving the poor. If not an organization, think of something you could do regularly that helps someone in need; it could be someone you know or a total stranger.

Read

Meditate on these verses:

- Read Galatians 6:1-18.
- Read Exodus 37:1-9 and Luke 24:1-9. Notice the mercy seat in both accounts. Jesus *is* the mercy seat. Even the angels like those on the Ark of the Covenant are present in the tomb.
- Read Hebrews 13:1-17.
- Read Deuteronomy 15:7-11.
- Read 1 Samuel 2:8-9.
- Read Luke 7:18-23.

Listen

- "Wonderful Merciful Savior" by Selah, *Press On*
- "Worthy Is the Lamb" by Brooklyn Tabernacle Choir, *I'll Say Yes*
- "O Come to the Altar" by Elevation Worship, *Here As in Heaven*
- "Never Alone" by Hilary Weeks, *The Collection*

CHAPTER 7

BLESSED ARE THE PURE IN HEART

"Look with wonder at the depth of the Father's marvelous love that he has lavished on us! He has called us and made us his very own beloved children. The reason the world doesn't recognize who we are is that they didn't recognize him. Beloved, we are God's children right now; however, it is not yet apparent what we will become. But we do know that when it is finally made visible, we will be just like him, for we will see him as he truly is. And all who focus their hope on him will always be purifying themselves, just as Jesus is pure."

— 1 JOHN 3:1-3, TPT

It's a peculiar thing when studying Scriptures, especially the Sermon on the Mount, that Jesus' focus is always on the hearts of men. It's so opposite of a world that exalts intellect, power, and position. And, being part of this world, we too tend to look at the Scriptures through an intellectual gaze, trying to make sense of every stroke of the pen. Our Lord's thoughts and ways are so far above our own because He is ever looking for the source of all of our evil so that He might cleanse our vessel from all sinful actions, thoughts and words.

Jesus delighted in the knowledge that one day we would grow up and become His holy habitation, that He could come and abide and dwell in us. He anticipated that we would become people of prayer, and that in our quiet times, He'd deposit secrets and mysteries from His heart to ours. He would open His Word to us and cause us to hear and see things nobody else saw or heard. He would speak life to us! That is why it delights Him to have a people "unto Himself." He calls us His priesthood, His body, His beloved, and His bride. His secrets are with the righteous because He is preparing a spotless bride for Himself.

The Sermon on the Mount begins with the benediction, *"Blessed are the poor in spirit,"* for Christ was dealing with men's spirits, their inner and spiritual nature. As we move on down this narrow path, we now encounter, *"Blessed are the pure in heart, for they shall see God"* (Matthew 5:8). This one strikes the very center of the target in which our Lord is after—the heart. Whatever "religion" may recognize as its adherent, a man whose heart is impure will not hold up under the gospel of God's Kingdom. If we say our heart is pure but our actions speak otherwise, it will nullify this purity we are declaring about ourselves.

People are always looking at external purities, which is why we esteem people better than we ought most times. God is always looking at the inner purity of our hearts, which is why—even more so today—I look upon present-day theologians and say, "Answer me, theologians reasoning out my theology, are you pure in heart? Has God's righteousness being imparted into your lives making you pure?" More than once, I've heard offensive, impure words coming from a pulpit towards unsuspecting sheep. We must be careful here, Church, because impurity of heart can cause spiritual blindness. Let's be sure we are not following a blind, hypocritical shepherd.

Purification of the heart admits us to a most glorious place. We shall see God! This purification is a divine operation wrought by the Holy

Lord Himself. It's interesting to note that this beatitude involves sight. We have already looked at the warnings given to the church of Laodicea. One reason they could not see their own nakedness was because spiritual blindness is the fruit of impurity. Such are people who have difficulty with alcoholism; they cannot see clearly. Their vision is often distorted or doubled. There are moral beauties and immoral horrors that certain people cannot see because they are impure in heart. This is why we must be "wise as serpents and harmless of doves" today in regards to those from whom we are receiving our theology. If we cannot discern the moral from the immoral, we too will be caught naked.

There is nothing more central to the Lord's teaching than the state of our hearts. Find any problem on the face of the earth, and you will find its root in the heart. In terrorism, you find the root of lies and deception. In fornication, you find the root of lust. In perfectionism, you find the root of fear. In rebellion, you find the root of witchcraft. In addiction, you may find roots of abuse, shame, rejection, and abandonment. All of our troubles arise out of the human heart. No matter how educated, connected, or wealthy you are, there is a root in your heart that either confirms you are a vessel of God being used for honor or denies you are a vessel of God being deceived and used for dishonor.

It is out of our heart that our mouth speaks. From our heart spring the issues of life. If not rooted in Christ, the issues of the heart manifest in our lives and the world. The abused becomes an abuser, the neglected because a victim, the person who feels abandoned by God becomes an atheist, the insecure person may use control as a means to feel empowered, and on and on it goes. We have a world full of people who are casualties of war.

However, the Christian heart is not immune to this either. We must guard our hearts from impurity because various sins can creep in.

When we allow the sin of covetousness, idolatry, false humility, self-righteousness, and others blind us, we can no longer look on our Lord as we used to. Our eyes will be blinded to the brightness of the glory of His being, and like looking into the sun, we will have to look away.

Reflect and Respond

- We have to ask the Lord to reveal blind spots in our lives because we can't see them! Ask Him now. Can you identify them? If so, journal what they are? What do you believe He is showing you about them?
- The condition of your heart should be in a much purer state than when you began this study. Describe the transformation you are noticing in your heart from beginning this study until now.

Wolves in Sheep's Clothing

Yes, God is going to shake everything that can be shaken. He is especially going to shake the Church because He wants the remnant to have a pure heart. He will not allow His bride to be mixed with the impure any longer, which is why so many of us are restless and unsatisfied. We're beginning to feel the shaking.

There are teachers within the Church today who are reviling the Word of God, watering down its doctrine, and attempting to blunt the sharpness of its message. When people speak against the gospel, it's because the gospel is speaking against them. They don't like the moral standard it holds them to. They will take a gospel truth and twist its meaning or judgment regarding a particular sin in order to justify their own impurity. We see this often when churches advertise in rather large signage, "All are welcome!" While it may be genuinely saying that anyone, no matter how sinful, is welcome to their church, it can carry another message: "Love God and keep your sin." How do I know this? I've met with some of the pastors of these churches and discerned within mere minutes that they were not following the gospel of God's Kingdom. Again, impurity equals spiritual blindness. He who has an ear, let Him hear what the Spirit is saying.

Sin always finds us out: *"You have sinned against the Lord; and be sure your sin will find you out"* (Numbers 32:23). We must be careful that we are not walking around with a dark lantern deceiving ourselves. People are really struggling today with moral and spiritual truths. They simply cannot understand the gospel of Christ. In most cases, it's their sin that prevents them from understanding it. The world says, "Go this way," and our Lord says, "Come with Me." If we're not careful, we'll forget our position of "He" and "I," and the created beings that we are will begin questioning the Creator and changing the gospel.

We begin making excuses for why sin is okay and should be tolerated. Whether we realize it or not, when we justify our sin, we are making a mockery of the cross. The atoning work of Christ on the cross can never be fully appreciated until a man's heart is rectified. We have never felt the weight of sin nor seen the blackness of it the way Christ has. The prophet Daniel tells us, *"He knows what is in the darkness and light dwells with Him"* (2:22). If you have ever been broken/brokenhearted because you have been terribly defiled by sin, then perhaps you, more than others, understand God's necessity for providing atonement. The atoning work of the cross is exactly what this world needed and still needs today. We do not need people telling us it's okay to stay in our sin. That is the blind leading the blind. We need the sword of God's Word to do a spiritual operation in us, to root out our sin, and show us that He's already nailed it to the cross.

New Creations

When we recognize the importance of atonement, we understand the need for regeneration, being born again. I struggled with this terminology when I was younger. I grew up in a religious home, raised in a particular denomination. The phrase "born again" was never discussed. When I was older, one of my nieces, middle school at the time, began telling me about being born again. I told her I believed in Jesus, His death on the cross, and that He died for my sins. What I didn't understand then, that I do now, is that it was all from my head, not from a place of regeneration. I was telling my niece what I knew to be true based on my theology and intellect at the time. It wasn't until many years later—years of God sending countless people into my life to plant and water seeds of truth—that I realized this magnificent truth somewhere in the middle of Kentucky driving home from my parents 50th anniversary party. The veil went off, and I could see…God.

We must become new creations in order to "see" our Lord. Our old nature, which includes our mind and heart, deceives us. As the Holy Spirit begins to convict us, our hearts cry out to be delivered. We recognize our jealousies, murders, rebellion, and evils of every kind. We cannot see our own impurity without Holy Spirit conviction. But, after we become a new creation, the Holy Spirit continues to reveal what hasn't yet been healed or brought into alignment with His nature, and we again cry out for deliverance.

Some people with unchanged or impure hearts may be struck with the beauty or purity of Christ's life, but those with a pure regenerated heart are enamored by it. We see that He's divine; He's too big to box in. When our hearts are pure in this way, we can see the great truths of the gospel through His spiritual lens, not a man-made intellectual one. When we are simple-minded (not lost in a sea of theological jargon), honest, sincere, and child-like in our faith, we enter into His kingdom with a door flung wide open. Matthew 18:3, says, *"Assuredly, I say to you, unless you are converted and become as little children, you will by no means enter the kingdom of heaven."* This causes me to tremble, and yet I know we must become as children before our Lord.

We are called to walk through the gates of righteousness. God's righteousness is not something we obtain from books or preachers but by going to His Word, sitting at His feet, and trusting in His name. Following the life of Christ is difficult. The early Church walked a difficult road; they prayed and fasted together and followed Him closely. Real revival swept through a culture that was not only ruled by a massive godless empire but also influenced by various religions. That encourages me today as the world becomes increasingly intolerant. I am beginning to see the pattern of what is happening. We started out with a pure gospel but soon became divided through religious institutions and doctrines of men; now, the Church is finding its way back to the simple truth of the life of Christ. He's getting His bride ready.

As we travel down this narrow path, let us also be careful of one other thing—formalism. It emphasizes ritual and observance over meaningfulness and is closely related to legalism. Charles Spurgeon defines it this way:

> It always looks to the shell, it never gets to the kernel. For formalism licks the bone but never gets to the marrow. It heaps to itself ceremonies, mostly of its own invention. And when it has attended to these it flatters itself that all is well, even though the heart itself still lusts after sin. The widows house is being devoured even at the very time when the Pharisee is making long prayers in the synagogue. Such a man cannot see God.

People operating with this trait will open the Bible, not to find what it says but to back up their own views and opinions. If the text they want is not there, other Scriptures will be found to twist in order to get their point across. The Bible becomes like a lump of wax that they mold to any shape they please. This is called proof-texting, manipulating Scripture to say what you want it to say to justify your man-made beliefs. Those who do this don't want to see the truth, so they don't.

Remember, Christ died outside the gate. He was anything but formal, ritualistic, or legalistic. When He taught, He said, "You have heard it said, but I say…" because He was reinterpreting Scripture, correcting the rabbinic formalism the people had been taught and helping them see God's abundant life in God's laws. When we seek *Him*—not formalism—we will find Him, when we seek Him with all of our heart.

Reflect and Respond

- How complex do you make the gospel? Do you rely on teachers to constantly teach you or on the Holy Spirit to teach you?
- Would you describe yourself as having child-like faith? Describe.

He's Coming Quickly

The Church that receives Christ's return will not be the Church we see today with its strobe lights and stages or processions and sages. Those are but outward apparel to draw us in and keep us in. No, the Church at the time of Christ's return will be a broken Church, broken for Him. It will be a praying, humble, fasting people who have emptied themselves, who study the Word of God, and who are filled with His mercy and purity. We will find ourselves, like the early Church, with empires against us, intolerant of our religious beliefs.

The communist governments of China and Russia tried to silence their people by removing their Bibles and places of worship. They didn't realize that their oppression became the spark that ignited a sleeping giant—a Church set on fire for Christ. What will it take to set the Church of America on fire? What will it take to wake this sleeping giant? Perhaps it will take losing everything to realize we had everything we needed all along, for Christ is all we need.

God is purifying His church. He's revealing Himself to those who are surrendering their whole life to Him. He's waking up the Body and speaking to both the old and the young. He'll speak to whoever is willing to posture themselves before Him in poverty of spirit and allow Him to completely take over their being. He'll use the unsuspecting person, whom the world does not know, to cast out demons, heal the sick, and bind up the brokenhearted because He can trust them and they believe He is who He says He is. They have become pure in heart, extending His mercy to many. The pure in heart hears God's footsteps everywhere, in the garden of the earth and the cool of the day. They will hear God's voice in tempest as hurricanes and fires rage. They will see God's hand in the heavens through the sun, moon, and stars and say, "Speak, Lord, I'm listening." The pure in heart will see God in the volcanoes and earthquakes because they trust His Word, *"He looks on the earth, and it trembles; He touches the hills, and they smoke"* (Psalm 104:32). Once the heart is right, God can be seen everywhere.

I enjoy watching for the signs of the Lord's return upon the earth. I study the Scriptures, I watch the things He says to watch and send out notes to whoever will listen, announcing the next incredible sign that appears. He's speaking loudly today. Some people receive it and are watching also. We share our excitement together, but many don't see it. They believe it's another hoax designed to deceive.

In the parable of the wise and foolish virgins (Matthew 25:1-13), the Lord delayed His return as the ten virgins were waiting for Him All were believers because they were all waiting for their Bridegroom,

Jesus Christ. Yet only half were watching and had their oil lamps full. They were prepared even though they fell asleep. They recognized the cry at midnight and ran to meet Him. Oh, Church, when your heart is right with God, you can see Him everywhere, you can even *see* Him speaking: *"I will...**watch** to see what He will say to me"* (Habakkuk 2:1*)*. We must be watching for our Lord in our everyday surroundings. Don't be blind. Pursue holiness *"without which no one will see the Lord"* (Hebrews 12:14).

"Blessed are the pure in heart, for they shall see God."

Practical Practices

Chapter 7

Church

Write your findings in a journal or notepad.

Carefully observe the teachings in your church this week. Be sure to write down every Scripture used and then go home and study them. Line up how the verses were used in church with what God is showing you about those Scriptures.

Every church should always welcome everyone, but we shouldn't depend on an announcement to communicate that. They should experience a warm welcome because of God's mercy and compassion manifested through us. Regardless of that, take the spiritual temperature of your church. Are people sitting there comfortably in their sin because sin is not being addressed or is sin being addressed?

Home

Is it hard for you to believe the Lord is returning for His people? Why?

Who do you rely on to teach you about such things? Is that person's heart pure? How do you know? What evidence do you have of that?

Do you watch the signs the Lord says to watch from Matthew 24:1-44, Mark 13, and Luke 21?

Take time every day this next week to notice every place you "see" God speaking to you. Spend time in nature, observe people, look at the heavens, read about earthquakes, volcanoes, and other "natural disasters." Journal all the ways you see God.

Read

Meditate on these verses:

- Read Hebrews 12:1-29
- Read Job 22:21-30.
- Read Proverbs 22:11.

Listen

- "Let the Weight of Your Glory" by Paul Wilbur, *Jerusalem Arise*
- "For Your Name Is Holy" by Paul Wilbur, *Jerusalem Arise*
- "Flood the Earth" by Katie Torwalt, Jesus Culture, *Love Has a Name*
- "Spirit Break Out" by Kim Walker-Smith, *Still Believe (Live)*

CHAPTER 8

BLESSED ARE THE PEACEMAKERS

"Pursue peace with all people, and holiness, without which no one will see the Lord."

— HEBREWS 12:14

The Beatitudes remind us that the outworking in the Christian life is altogether different than everything else known by man who is not Christian. This becomes very obvious in the seventh beatitude: *"Blessed are the peacemakers, for they shall be called sons of God"* (Matthew 5:9). Becoming a man or woman of peace is a result of the supernatural inner working of God's sanctification within us. We must die, get alone, hunger and thirst, become merciful and then pure. It's only natural that the next place we land on this path is in becoming peaceable, for we cannot seek the peace that Christ seeks without first having a pure heart in which to operate this peace from.

As children of God, we find that we carry dual citizenship. We are citizens of the country in which God placed us on the earth, and we are citizens of His Kingdom. We are in a very unique position, for although we are *in* the world, we are no longer *of* it. This means it's possible, with Christ's nature in us, to bring a supernatural peace to a world that is seeking a worldly peace. We must set our faces like flint against everything that is contrary to God and His holiness and do it in such a manner that we remain peaceable. But no matter how peaceable we are, we shall still be misrepresented and misunderstood. Jesus Himself, the Prince of Peace, was despised and rejected though He loved all mankind. We can expect no less, but that shouldn't stop us from being a peacemaker.

Soldiers are made, not born. God is carefully working in the secret place to refine a bride and build up an army. Only His army is one whose sword is His Word, whose shield is their God, and whose countenance is peace. Though peacemakers look like all other people, we are distinguished by His character. We have a desire to maintain peace whether in our homes, our communities, the workplace, or anywhere else we find ourselves. We are sensitive to what others think and feel and try to conduct our conversations and relations accordingly. Right now, people are easily provoked, and so, more than ever, we need to be exercising a spirit of peace in every place. We can all relay stories of family members, friends, or acquaintances who have reacted passionately—maybe irately—over certain topics, be it war, guns, schools, immigration, abortion, or many other social issues. If God called us onto this path and has brought us this far, He must trust us to behave as peacemakers when we find ourselves in strained and strange dialogue.

He knows that *"a servant of the Lord must not quarrel but be gentle to all, able to teach, patient, in humility correcting those who are in opposition, if God perhaps will grant them repentance, so that they may know the truth, and that they may come to their senses and escape the snare of the devil, having been taken captive by him to do his will"*

(2 Timothy 2:24-26). Friends, we should desire an outcome of peace in every situation we are in and every conversation we have. This Scripture tells us that God desires those who are not walking with Him to know the truth. He wants them to come to their senses and escape the captivity and lies of the enemy. They have spiritual blindness and are unable to see things the way you and I see them.

This is why we must stay in constant prayer and why God gives us specific prayer assignments. He knows where the hard hearts are hidden and wants the seed of His word implanted in them. If we allow ourselves to be derailed by our old nature at times we could be sowing good seed and peace is not evident, we'll hear what many of us hear, "They call themselves a Christian? Hypocrite!"

God is raising up holy men and women in this hour who will be Spirit born, Spirit directed, Spirit authorized, and Spirit energized. He conducts His operation with those of a pure heart because having a pure heart creates a peacemaker like Jesus Christ. As a peacemaker, you will have an entirely new view of mankind. You will see people as victims of Satan's schemes and have pity and mercy on them. You will only have one concern—the glory of God among men. Jesus was not interested in glorifying Himself; His one concern was bringing glory to His Father. God's peacemakers are men or women whose central concern is no longer to bring glory to self but giving glory to God. They will spend the rest of their lives trying to minister to that glory. When they see individual or international disputes and quarreling, they see it distracting from the glory of God, and out of that concern, they pursue peace.

When a famous physic was holding an event at a local entertainment venue in town, I could not just sit and do nothing while people were being drawn into deception and witchcraft. The first time this person came, I was warned; the second time, God sent me to the venue to eat dinner. I did not realize that this person was the scheduled "event" for the night. Like Paul when the demonic slave girl was following him, I was greatly annoyed. Who dares to steal God's glory and boast of a counterfeit supernatural experience? Peace needed to be restored.

The event was not only trying to steal God's glory; it was also going to rob innocent people of any kind of peace they thought they had, but they didn't know that. They were sheep being led to the slaughter. It took every ounce of restraint in me not to open the doors of the party room and interrupt the calling up of familiar spirits. We are strictly warned in Scripture about familiar spirits and that we are not to even entertain the idea of calling them up (Leviticus 19:31). I prayed in the lobby, regrouped, and maintained a spirit of peace. I didn't interrupt the room but rather called on God's special forces, the intercessors! We stormed heaven from every angle we could so that all dark knowledge would become foolishness. Peacemakers understand that they don't always have to engage in direct confrontation; they understand the importance of covert operations being done through a spirit of peace.

Reflect and Respond

- Think about a time you were involved in an event, a party you found yourself at, or a situation that you knew was completely against the nature of God and that other people would be affected by it. What did you do? How did you respond?
- What would you do differently, knowing what you know about God now?

His Word Is Pure

The first thing evident in a person who is being transformed into a peacemaker is that he is able to hold his tongue. *"Let every man be swift to hear, slow to speak, slow to wrath"* (James 1:19). A peacemaker learns not to speak. When we are being pushed for a reply or baited into a conversation designed to trap us, we hold our tongue. Our tongues can do great harm. *"Even so the tongue is a little member and boasts great things. See how great a forest a little fire kindles"* (James 3:5). For the sake of peace, we must control our tongue, not just in situations or with others but even when speaking about ourselves.

Peacemakers also learn to measure everything against Scripture. Jesus came against the schemes of the devil with the Word of God when He was tempted in the wilderness. He used it to rebuke the Pharisees, cast out demons, teach in the synagogues, heal the sick, and honor God's law in every way. Everything He did aligned with the written Word. He never had to argue because His greatest weapon was His own words, the words of His Kingdom, which spoke truth, overruling the lies used in the kingdom of darkness.

"For the word of God is living and powerful, and sharper than any two-edged sword, piercing even to the division of soul and spirit, and of joints and marrow, and is a discerner of the thoughts and intents of the heart. And there is no creature hidden from His sight, but all things are naked and open to the eyes of Him to whom we must give account" (Hebrews 4:12-13). No creature is hidden from His sight! We have to learn how to use the Word of God in every situation we find ourselves in because it overrules the kingdom of Satan. God's Word may have the sting of a cut at first, but it brings truth, and truth sets us free from Satan's lies.

One day I offered a woman a ride home because her car had stalled in the grocery store parking lot. On the drive home, we talked about all kinds of things: dogs, skiing, Colorado, family. I learned that she owned a marijuana dispensary and was in a homosexual marriage. We didn't skip a beat in our conversation, although inside myself, I did chuckle at how funny God can be. She told me that I'll have good "karma" for taking her home. I replied, "Actually, I don't believe in karma. I'm a Christian, and I'd love to pray for you before I drop you off if that's okay with you." She agreed! I pulled in her driveway and proceeded to pray *His Word* over her. I prayed His truth concerning her life. Before she left the car, she gave me a quick hug and said, "Carole, you're not like other Christians. Most Christians wouldn't act like this towards me."

Rather than her words puffing me up, they were like a knife to my heart. I drove home so deeply grieved for the body of Christ and how people see us, myself, too, on many occasions. They don't see us as peacemakers but peace takers. That's what needs to change, which only comes when we die to self, mourn over sin, become meek, hunger for Him, get filled with His mercy, and have our hearts purified. Then and only then can we walk in the kind of authority and peace as Christ did upon the earth.

I was not ashamed to tell this woman I didn't believe in karma. I did not sow karma; I sowed into God's Kingdom. *"Do not be deceived: God cannot be mocked. A man reaps what he sows. Whoever sows to please their flesh, from the flesh will reap destruction; whoever sows to please the Spirit, from the Spirit will reap eternal life"* (Galatians 6:7-8, NIV). We must learn to sow peace by speaking truth, God's Word, in love.

God's Word has been around since the beginning; it's the constitution of His Kingdom. His Kingdom has authority on the earth, which means everything else must yield to it. The kingdom of darkness *is* subject to the Kingdom of Light! When we pray His Word over situations, we pray in faith, believing, because we're praying the King's words right back to Him…now He must act. That's why His disciples could cast out demons. They commanded them "in the name of the King" to come out. A king must act on any words He has spoken. Kings and queens rarely speak because when they do, it becomes law, and once it's law, they must follow through with what is now written.

If the body of Christ understood this and knew how to use God's Word to fight the spiritual forces of wickedness in the heavenly places, things would look a lot different in our communities and nations. We need to realize that our Bibles are the King's words. I want to pray for anyone I can because I know that when I pray His Word over them, then God will act on it. When my new friend said "yes" to prayer, I knew when I prayed for her, the ball was now in God's court. I prayed, believing, and had peace, not because I saw an immediate result, but because I knew God would now act on His Word.

Friends, we need to stop fighting with people. This battle we're in is against spiritual forces of darkness. Paul explains this very clearly in Ephesians 6:12: *"For we do not wrestle against flesh and blood, but against principalities, against powers, against the rulers of the darkness of this age..."* Look past the person and see what's really in operation behind the scenes. God wants you to see people from His angle. He knows what lies in the darkness. He sees things you can't see about that person. It's our responsibility as "the church" to understand what we're really coming against and bring peace into the midst of chaos.

I'm perplexed some days how many of us can sit idly by while the world pulls further and further away from truth. In case we are in danger of forgetting, hell has no exits, and every day thousands are finding themselves there. We must bring truth peacefully, not with hatred, anger, argument, or judgmentalism.

Reflect and Respond

- Write down in your journal on a scale of 1-10 how knowledgeable you are in Scripture. It's not a condemnation, just an assessment from which to start.
- Make a new mark where you would like to be. (If you assessed yourself at 5, would you like to be at 6 or 8?) Pray and ask God to help you get there.
- If you have been a Christian a long time and believe you know the Word well, ask God to take you even deeper and challenge you to learn other Scriptures that are not yet in your arsenal. Ask the Holy Spirit to help you set a goal.

A Unified Body

Going across a ship to America with Mr. Oglethorpe, who was to be the governor of Savannah, John Wesley heard a great noise in the future governor's cabin. Mr. Wesley went to the cabin to look into the matter. Mr. Oglethorpe shared with him that the only wine he liked to drink was Cypress wine, that it was necessary for him. He put it on board the ship only to find his servant, Grimaldi, had drunken all of it. He was to have him beaten on the deck and then delivered to the first war ship of His majesty that was destined to come by. This boy, Oglethorpe said, will know that "I never forgive." "Your honor," said Mr. Wesley, "then I hope you never sin." The rebuke stuck right where it was intended. The governor replied, "I do sin, and I have sinned in what I have said. For your sake, he shall be forgiven."

As peacemakers, we must remember how the Lord forgave us. Mr. Wesley gently and peaceably reminded Mr. Oglethorpe, and it had the affect God intended—repentance. This also shows the importance of unity within the body of Christ. We must learn to hold each other accountable to living a life with Christ's nature in us. Anything else is not acceptable. Unity of spirit is an outward manifestation of peacemakers. They are of one accord.

Today, many people in the body of Christ differ in their theology and can make it a heated point of contention, but if are governed by God's Word, we should be able to maintain a spirit of peace. Take healing for example. Rather than argue about how we should or shouldn't respond to someone in need of healing, we should look upon our brother or sister in Christ in a spirit of peace and unity with the same mercy Christ shared for the sick. God chooses the outcome, but in faith, we pray God's words and release the action to our King.

Paul writes, *"fulfill my joy by being like-minded, having the same love, being of one accord, of one mind"* (Philippians 2:2). Unity must be a blessed thing for Paul to labor so much for it. Let us be at peace in our different denominations and put away our swords for a while. Strife arose between Abraham's herdsmen and Lot's herdsmen, but Abraham handled it peacefully. *"Please, let there be no strife between you and me, and between my herdsmen and your herdsmen; for we are brethren. Is not the whole land before you? Please separate from me. If you take the left, then I will go to the right; or, if you go to the right, then I will go to the left"* (Genesis 13: 8-9). A peacemaker strives for peace at all times, especially in the church. We should want to bind the believers together so that they are one in Christ. This way the world will know that the Father has sent His Son into the world, heralded with the song, *"Glory to God in the highest and on earth peace, goodwill toward men"* (Luke 2:14).

When we learn to listen more than we speak, and then learn to use God's Word and measure everything in light of His Word, we will notice so many more opportunities around us to practice being peacemakers. We are already working on our selflessness daily so God can operate more fully. God is filling us with His mercy and purifying us daily so the outward flow of peace is coming more naturally as we are becoming more approachable, lovable, sympathetic, and understanding. As a result, He calls us "children of God." It means we are becoming more like our Father. I love that. I am taking on God's character, and His nature is being manifested in me. As this become more noticeable, people will want what we have!

Remember that Jesus humbled Himself and counted it not robbery to be equal with God. He asks no less of you. Humble yourself. That's our first beatitude—being poor in spirit. We have, in fact, seen Jesus in all of them. He grieves over sin, He's meek, He hungered and thirsted for His Father and sought Him fervently in prayer. He was filled with mercy and purity and was known as the Prince of Peace. He did not hang on to His deity but humbled Himself even to death. He did all of this because He wasn't thinking of Himself. He was thinking of you and me.

To be a peacemaker is to no longer think about yourself. You lay down the need to be right. You are no longer easily offended and have zero desire to win a ridiculous argument. You begin to think of others above yourself, *"Let nothing be done through selfish ambition or conceit, but in lowliness of mind let each esteem others better than himself"* (Philippians 2:3). You finish with self and begin to follow Jesus.

"Purge me, prune me, correct me, grow me, teach me, show me…" are words that I've prayed regularly over the years in my prayer time. I want no part of my former self or my natural self. I'm willing to do whatever He wants me to do so that people no longer see me; they see our Lord. When I pour myself out to our Father, I find that all of the Beatitudes flood into perfect order. There truly is nothing like Kingdom order. The moment my heart bows in prayer, I can barely look up because the weight of His presence immediately floods my being. I am fully aware of His kingdom within me and the obedience

His kingdom requires. Remember, it's the poor in spirit that inherit the Kingdom of God, and when we are positioned in such a manner, His presence becomes obvious.

"Blessed are the peacemakers, for they shall be called children of God."

PRACTICAL PRACTICES

CHAPTER 8

Church

Write your findings in a journal or notepad.

Try to visit a different church this month to receive a different perspective on your theology. Observe where it's difficult for you to be a peacemaker in this environment.

Home

In your prayers this week, ask God to purge you, prune you, correct you, and teach you. It's hard to get the words out at first, but He will do exactly as you ask and reveal even deeper truths to you.

Ask the Holy Spirt to show you where you are not at peace within the body of Christ. What theology (the Holy Spirit, healing, demonstrative worship, etc.) do you struggle with?

Why do you think it is so difficult to unify the body of Christ? Explain.

Read

Meditate on these verses:

- Read Genesis 13:1-9.
- Read Psalm 34:1-22.

- Read Isaiah 9:1-8.
- Read Haggai 2:6-9.
- Read John 14:25-31.

Listen

- "My Prayer" by Alberto & Kimberly Rivera, *The Father Sings*
- "Fill Me Up" by Jesus Culture, *Awakening: Live in Chicago*
- "My Inheritance" by Travis Cottrell, *Jesus Saves*
- "Amazing Grace" by Darlene Zschtech, *Timeless Hymns of Faith*

CHAPTER 9

BLESSED ARE THE PERSECUTED

"The early church was married to poverty, prisons and persecutions. Today, the church is married to prosperity, personality, and popularity."

— LEONARD RAVENHILL

"You can discern the face of the sky and of the earth, but how is it you do not discern this time?" (Luke 12:56). One of the biggest aches in my heart right now is that as believers we are ill-equipped for what is coming. Everything we know is going to get turned on its head, and barely a sermon is preached on it. We do not understand the times in which we live, and as a result, we have no sense of urgency for the hour. We should be fasting and weeping, but we are eating, drinking, and living as though we have not a care in the world.

Issachar was one of the twelve tribes of Israel. God called them anointed men *"who know how to interpret the signs of the times"* (1 Chronicles 12:32, TLV). Oh, how we need people with the Issachar anointing right now! As they discerned the times and seasons in which they lived, they knew that their only hope was in the God of Israel. My friends, the God of Israel is still our only hope. He is the same yesterday, today, and forever. He was made flesh and tabernacled among us, and His name is Jesus Christ, Yeshua HaMashiach (in Hebrew). He is our only source of hope and strength in this hour.

Jerusalem is becoming the burdensome stone it was prophesied to be (Zechariah 12:3), the nations are raging, the heavens are speaking, the earth is in labor, and the depravity of mankind is increasing. There is only one power on the earth that can withstand the onslaught of evil that is invading the earth—the Church of Jesus Christ anointed with the Holy Ghost. Prophetic Scriptures are playing out before our very eyes, but rather than examine the Scriptures ourselves to find out what God is saying, we're relying on Christian leaders to tell us what is happening in the world. I look for those leaders today, and they are far and few between. The devil sure has done a number on the bride of Christ.

Persecution of the Righteous

We come now to the top of this ladder we are climbing to become salt, light, and a city on a hill. We have been taking a deep journey with the Lord along the narrow path and have come to a climatic finish: *"Blessed are those who are persecuted for righteousness sake, for theirs is the kingdom of heaven"* (Matthew 5:10). Who are these righteous that will be persecuted? *"Yes, and all who desire to live godly in Christ Jesus will suffer persecution"* (2 Timothy 3:12). We cannot escape. *All* Christians will suffer persecution. But Christ calls us "blessed." We're considered blessed because it says to the world, "We're the salt of the earth. Now we're shaking the world and warring for the people." This should make us rejoice. *"Blessed are you when they revile and persecute you, and say all kinds of evil against you falsely for My sake. Rejoice and be exceedingly glad, for great is your reward in heaven, for so they persecuted the prophets who were before you"* (Matthew 5:11-12).

Though persecution is inevitable, we may ask the Lord, "Why must it be?" The answer is only because we're righteous. We have seen that there are two types of righteousness the Bible speaks of: *imputed* righteousness we receive when we are born again and *imparted* righteousness we receive during the process of sanctification. This beatitude speaks of imparted righteousness. We'll never be persecuted for righteousness imputed. Rather, the world will see Jesus in your sanctified self and want to crucify Him all over again.

As a result of our being made pure in heart towards God and man, the world will begin to persecute us because our life condemns them. They will notice people around them no longer walking in sin. That's you and me, and we make them feel uncomfortable. Misery loves company, but when the company leaves and is no longer miserable, misery becomes like an obsessive jilted lover who will not rest until they see the righteous pay for making them feel more miserable. God allows them to persecute us because they're under the conviction of the Holy Spirit, and that is the first step to saving their souls!

Another result of righteousness imparted is we become the light of the world. Put a light in darkness, friend, and everyone will see it. *"Let your light so shine before men, that they may see your good works and glorify your Father in heaven"* (Matthew 5:16). When they "see" your good works, some will ask about the light and the hope that is in you. Then you can be bold in giving them an account of your life so that all glory goes to the work of Christ in your life. In this way, our lives fulfill the law of God, *"Do not think that I came to destroy the Law or the Prophets. I did not come to destroy but to fulfill"* (Matthew 5:17).

Reflect and Respond

- What is your opinion about those who watch for the return of Christ? Explain why you believe that.
- What have you been taught about law and grace? What do you currently believe? Explain.

The Law Written on Our Hearts

Don't stoop once God has made you righteous. Don't stoop to the statement that "I am under the dispensation of grace, not under the bondage of law." Most people who say that end up *in disgrace*. Christ Himself says He didn't come to destroy the law, but to fulfill it in and through your life when you absolutely surrender to Him and He has control. We don't fulfill the law through legalistic application where we have a set of rules hanging in front of our eyes or through discipline to follow those rules in our own strength. We are also not under bondage to Old Testament sacrificial or ceremonial laws because Jesus fulfilled those by His death on the cross.

Rather, once He got control of us, He wrote His laws on our hearts by His Spirit. Then we fulfill those laws in every circumstance, no matter how trying it may be, by spontaneously reacting without any effort of our own. This is why during persecution, we should not worry about what we'll say. *"But when they arrest you, do not worry about what to say or how to say it. At that time you will be given what to say, for it will not be you speaking, but the Spirit of your Father speaking through you"* (Matthew 10:19-20, NIV). In trials, we'll be able to react under the anointing of the Holy Spirit within us, fulfilling the law and bearing the fruit of the Spirit because the fruit of the Spirit is Christ! Holiness is Christ!

There's no other standard. Holiness is heresy if it's not Christ. The work of the Holy Spirit is to conform you into the image of the Son,

Jesus Christ. When God writes His laws upon our hearts and we spontaneously fulfill them because we're so completely surrendered to His will, filled with His Spirit, and now controlled by His Spirit, then we've yielded. There's no fight left and God takes control. Our lives are on the altar.

Friends, don't be deceived that there is no standard of holiness to live up to. There is, but it's not legalistic. We've been told by people who lack understanding that all law—even that which leads to holiness—is legalism. Christ cannot contradict Himself. He fulfilled the law, and our lives surrendered to Christ fulfill the law. We don't fulfill the law just a little bit but by the full standard. Many are teaching that "I'm under grace, not the law, so I can do anything," No, you are under a lie! You can't do anything you want because you are not your own anymore, and if you are not made holy, you are not under grace because Jesus Christ is all about making you holy. You are His temple, and He wants to abide in a *holy* temple.

New Voices

Bold new voices are being raised up in this hour because a storm is coming, and the Church is not prepared for it. Scripture tells us that when this trajectory hits us, many who have professed Christ will turn away. That should cause us to want to sit up and pay attention. Whether it's the first century or today, persecuted believers have become the new face of genuine Christianity, which is why I'm restless sitting in church listening to another sermon on the "issues" of the day. We need sermons on sin, the blood of Christ, atonement, eternity, spiritual warfare, the judgment seat of Christ, and how to prepare ourselves as His bride.

We are dying to live and not living to die. This present system of wickedness and corruption is coming to an end in a battle the earth has never seen, but the enemy will not go down without a fight. The last thing he wants is for the bride of Christ to see the Light of heaven, so he will deceive you, bewitch you, and lull you to sleep in complacency if he knows he can. He has already twisted the doctrine of sin, the Holy Spirit, Israel, law, prayer, and infallibility of Scripture with gullible men and women over the generations. Rather than let our Father show us what is truth, we believe every famous person that comes along who has a radio spot, pulpit, or television show.

He gave us the Holy Spirit to lead us into all truth. *"But the anointing* [the Holy Spirit] *which you have received from Him abides in you, and you do not need that anyone teach you; but as the same anointing teaches you concerning all things, and is true, and is not a lie, and just as it has taught you, you will abide in Him"* (1 John 2:27). The Holy Spirit teaches you…when you are abiding. Where does abiding start? It begins in the prostrated place of prayer, in becoming poor in spirit, and walking the narrow path of holiness in order to become a consecrated vessel.

It is in the name of the King that we go against the multitudes of darkness. It is at the name of Jesus Christ that every knee will bow in heaven, on the earth, and under the earth, and every tongue will confess that Jesus is Lord (Philippians 2:10-11). That must be the Church. We must confess that He is our Lord, no matter what comes our way. Scripture doesn't say we're persecuted because we're objectionable, difficult, or fanatical. It doesn't even say we're persecuted for a cause. It says we're persecuted for our righteousness.

When Christ's life is evident in your life, you are a walking rebuke to sin. People won't like who you are because you are living at a level of holiness they can't understand. They will call you intolerant, racist, homophobic or any other name they can come up with because they feel condemned by your presence. In their minds, they have already justified their sin according to the world's standard of living, and the world loves its own.

When they see righteousness in you, it means you are a poured out, meek vessel, and God is filling you with Himself, so technically they are not persecuting you; they are persecuting Him. Jesus told us to expect this: *"If the world hates you, know that it has hated Me before you. If you were of the world, the world would love you as its own. But you are not of the world, since I have chosen you out of the world; therefore the world hates you"* (John 15:18-19, TLV). You are not of this world anymore. That is what God is trying to get through to each of us. You are part of His Kingdom even though you still have dual citizenship at the moment. His kingdom lives in you so naturally the kingdom of darkness is going to hate the Kingdom of Light.

God wants you to experience holy, consecrated living because He wants to exercise His Kingdom power and authority through you to help others in the earth see Him. God wants to move you out of your "experiential" Christian living, where you look for one experience after the other, and move you into only needing Him. One day, our "experiences" are going to be gone, and all we will have is Him. We better start understanding that now.

Reflect and Respond

- What kind of shift are you feeling, if any, in the body of Christ?
- What draws you to present-day Christianity? Explain.

The Walking Wounded

By whom are the righteous persecuted? Scriptures and church history prove that it's not confined to the world. Some of the most grievous persecution has come at the hands of the Church itself and at the hands of other religious people. There is no denomination void of persecuting believers. The Lord was persecuted by Pharisees and scribes. The early Christians were persecuted by the Jews. The Roman Catholic Church persecuted many in the Middle Ages. Most persecution came from within the body of Christ. Many who just wanted to live a quiet, sincere life in the truth of Scripture experienced forced conversions, excommunications, and in many cases, death.

There are ideas of Christianity today that are far removed from New Testament teachings. They are causing persecution towards those who are trying to follow Christ on the narrow path. The body of Christ can be ruthless to its own. We have walking-wounded from many churches, Bible study groups, and other organizations. We have our own "trail of tears" within the body of Christ. I've seen and heard too much. I know too many people who have suffered at the hands of the "righteous," many of which are still operating behind the scenes in organizations today. We have to figure this out because God says judgment begins in the house of God first—that means you and me. We need to examine ourselves and how it is we're treating other believers. Whether someone is Charismatic or Pentecostal, Catholic or Lutheran, non-denominational or hosting a home church, we are all part of the body of Christ and Christ said the world will know us when we are One. We have some work to do.

Previously, we asked why Christians are persecuted and found that it's because we are righteous. Now, let's ask a slightly different question: Why are the righteous persecuted and not the *good or noble*? It's pretty straightforward. The good and noble represent an outward appearance of what people in the world think others should look like; therefore, they are "accepted" by the world and not persecuted. The righteous are persecuted because they are considered *different*. They live according to a standard of goodness and righteousness that looks different from the world's standards. The world cannot relate to these standards. That's because God is creating a new species of people, Kingdom people, and because there is nothing else like them on the face of the earth, they're different.

People do not know what to do with "different." They look at someone operating in the gifts of the Spirit, for example, and *it's different*, so it's bad. Someone walks barefoot for the cause of sex trafficking and is compared to a man traveling everywhere barefoot. People conclude that walking barefoot for a cause is "different," so it must be wrong. We can go to a prayer meeting at a home where everyone is on the floor travailing, groaning, or praying in the Spirit, and we leave early because *it's different*, so it's uncomfortable. We can be next to someone in church lifting their hands high and singing passionately. We squirm because *it's different*; it's not the "norm."

Yet, Jesus was *different.* There was something about Him that condemned the Pharisees and scribes. They felt the righteousness in Jesus Christ, and it made their righteousness look like filthy rags. After Lazarus was raised from the dead and walked the earth, his presence also condemned them, and they wanted to kill him too. Righteousness does not condemn in words but by the presence of God in us. Is that what is really making Christians uncomfortable with other Christians? Are the uncomfortable ones feeling the conviction that maybe there's more to God than they're allowing in their own life?

Leading by Example

There is no better chapter in the Bible that shows this than Hebrews 11. It vividly describes the life of people in Scripture who walked with such great faith in God that it was counted to them as righteousness. Not only were they different, they kept their eyes on the promises of God even though they never obtained those promises themselves, but the author of Hebrews tells us they will not be made perfect apart from us! Now keep in mind, if we think we have weird brothers and sisters in the faith now, wait until we're *all* together! We're talking about a man who spent years building a boat, an old woman having a baby, a guy that never died but just disappeared, and a father who was about to kill his son. We need to get over ourselves and quit boxing in our supernatural God. He's beyond comprehension. The Hebrews 11 patriarchs knew it and had faith to express it, even though it cost them dearly.

> …who through faith subdued kingdoms, worked righteousness, obtained promises, stopped the mouths of lions, quenched the violence of fire, escaped the edge of the sword, out of weakness were made strong, became valiant in battle, turned to flight the armies of the aliens. Women received their dead raised to life again. Others were tortured, not accepting deliverance, that they might obtain a better resurrection. Still others had trial of mockings and scourgings, yes, and of chains and imprisonment. They were stoned, they were sawn in two, were tempted, were slain with the sword. They wandered about in sheepskins and goatskins, being destitute, afflicted, tormented—of whom the world was not worthy. They wandered in deserts and mountains, in dens and caves of the earth. And all these, having obtained a good testimony through faith, did not receive the promise, God having provided something better for us, that they should not be made perfect apart from us. (Hebrews 11:33-39)

The world was not worthy of the righteous then, nor is it now, and it will continue that way until we are removed from the world. As I look at our brothers and sisters around the world starved to death in gulags, lit on fire in cages, beheaded over their profession of faith in Jesus Christ in the Middle East, silenced in our schools, and mocked on social media, I am reminded that this is the true call on our life. If Christ was hated because of His righteousness, we will be too. Are you prepared for that kind of Christian living? Daniel was a righteous man who conducted his affairs with God in private; however, his outward righteousness spoke volumes, and a plot was devised to destroy him. I don't hear sermons preached about this much on Sunday mornings.

If our conception of Jesus Christ is that He can be admired and applauded by the non-Christian, we have a wrong view of Him. He was utterly hated because of His absolute righteousness, holiness, and truth. His contemporaries threw stones at Him and chose a murderer instead of Him, ultimately putting Him to death. Many will tell you they admire Jesus Christ: "He was an extraordinary man," or "He was a great prophet." That just tells you they don't really know Him. That's their way of making Him "acceptable" and minimizing how different Jesus Christ was and is. If they saw His righteousness and holiness, they would hate Him if that made them aware of their unrighteousness. Christ doesn't change, nor does man, so let's be careful that we don't make Him so "acceptable" that He's no longer in conflict with the world, for the world *will* hate righteousness.

Reflect and Respond

- Have you ever experienced being persecuted by another believer? Explain.
- Have you struggled with unforgiveness or bitterness as a result of this persecution?
- Take that to God now. Confess, release, and forgive.

Wake Up

In this study, we have been through deep self-examination. We examined what our life looks like being empty of self, filled with Him, and now being a rebuke to the world. Working through the Beatitudes is a daily self-examination designed to test what a real Kingdom Christian looks and acts like. Jesus spoke a hard word to His disciples that we need to take note of: *"Woe to you when all men speak well of you, for so did their fathers to the false prophets"* (Luke 6:26). Isn't is so true that our idea of what we call a perfect Christian nearly always is that he is a nice, popular man who never offends anyone and is so easy to get along with? But if this beatitude about being persecuted is true, then that is not a real Christian. The real Christian is someone who is *not* praised by everybody. They did not praise our Lord, and they will not praise the people who are like Him.

If we could peek into the door of heaven and see what God sees, we would change everything. God views eternity, and we're taught to be eternity conscious. I can't bear the thought of anyone going to hell, not even the worse criminal. We can't waste our time worrying about anything else except being clothed in righteousness because that is our garment in heaven:

> And I heard, as it were, the voice of a great multitude, as the sound of many waters and as the sound of mighty thunderings, saying, "Alleluia! For the Lord God Omnipotent reigns! Let us be glad and rejoice and give Him glory, for the marriage of the Lamb has come, and His wife has made herself ready." And to her it was granted to be arrayed in fine linen, clean and bright, for the fine linen is the righteous acts of the saints. (Revelation 19:6-8)

Our righteousness is the very material that makes up the garment we will be wearing at the marriage supper of the Lamb. We won't be clothed in good works, good intentions or good thoughts. We must be empty of ourselves so we can hunger for this kind of righteousness. As His mercy, purity, and peace are revealed in us, our works will then display His works and His will. Then we will be able to say with the psalmist, *"I will triumph in the works of Your hands"* (Psalm 92:4b).

To be a true Christian is to be like Christ, not the world. James tells us that friendship with world is "enmity" with God (James 4:4), meaning hostile towards God. I've mentioned that before but it bears repeating because many believers today still embrace this world and the things in it. It doesn't mean we can't enjoy the benefits of beauty or adventure, but to be like Christ means we are totally changed. Unfortunately, a lot of our old nature is still in us, which hates Christ and hates righteousness (Romans 8:6-8).

How else can you explain that when a believer walking in holiness comes along and challenges the status quo, the status quo Christian becomes offended? This happens in churches as leaders are building their own kingdom and in Bible studies when Christians talk the talk but do not walk the walk. We experience this kind of tension in our daily lives when we are challenged to come up higher. Some of us do not want to be challenged to holiness because we're gaining the acceptance and approval of man and it feels pretty darn good—except it's friendship with world. No, to truly become like Christ, we become light, which always exposes the darkness, and darkness hates light.

What does Jesus say of those who are persecuted? Whether we are persecuted by the world or persecuted by other believers in the church, we will inherit the Kingdom of Heaven. Isn't it interesting that the Beatitudes begin with becoming poor in spirit and, as a result, inheriting the Kingdom of Heaven, and then once we're filled with Him, we're persecuted but again inherit the Kingdom of Heaven? We start with the Kingdom of Heaven, and we end with it.

This is meant to impress upon us the importance of membership in the Kingdom of Heaven. The Jews had a false idea about the Kingdom and how to become part of it. Jesus was stating the complete opposite than what the Jews believed. He reminded His followers that they were of a *different* kingdom. There is no entrance to His Kingdom if we are full of self but once we're humbled and filled with His nature, we find that there is no entrance without some type persecution. It's the evidence of Christ living in us.

Persecutions are coming to the body of Christ, but mainly for those who are living righteously. There's still a lot of pride in the Church. Far too many of us still want to be "right" in our theology rather than letting the Bible and the Holy Spirit speak for themselves, which means we still have some emptying to do. I tell myself often, "The more I know, the less I know" because, as an avid seeker for truth, I have come to realize that He's unsearchable. It's when I hunger and thirst after righteousness—and not being "right"—that He deposits His nature and truth into my spirit. Then He brings a whole new level of revelation and understanding to His being and to His Word because His ways are not our ways.

I want to encourage you to be careful in exalting spiritual leaders. Yes, God has anointed people in various ways in order to "build up" the body of Christ, but we are not to worship any part of the body except the Head. God is seeing to that through His current season of unmasking. He is ripping the lid off the hidden sin of man in every avenue of life so that His glorious light can shine in and heal. *"For nothing is secret that will not be revealed, nor anything hidden that will not be known and come to light'* (Luke 8:17).

God does not want us putting our hope in a preacher, an actor, a politician, or anyone else, only in Him, so He's going to great lengths to show us that no one is immune from moral failure. The prophet Zechariah says that, at some point, things are going to get so bad that we'll realize the only place to look for help is up! That's where God's taking us—up. He wants us to quit looking down at our phones and social media accounts, jam-packed schedules, and other distractions and just look up at Him. He must become all we need. Then may we cry out like King Asa did realizing that there was no one to help in the battle of the powerless against the mighty except the Living God.

> *And Asa cried out to the Lord his God, and said, "Lord, it is nothing for You to help, whether with many or with those who have no power; help us, O Lord our God, for we rest on You, and in Your name we go against this multitude. O Lord, You are our God; do not let man prevail against You!"* (2 Chronicles 14:11).

I'll never forget watching the 21 Egyptian Coptic Christians parading on the beach in their orange jumpsuits walking to their death. They were in a single file line with not an expression on their faces. I remember noticing more than anything else how calm they were. It was as if they had a steely resolve even though they knew in moments they would be decapitated. It was so Christlike. They weren't fighting to get away or screaming or acting out in any way. As they knelt down in front of their executioners, I couldn't watch anymore.

Church, get ready! Jesus is coming, and persecutions are going to increase. It doesn't necessarily mean we will be persecuted in the same manner as the Middle Eastern believers. There's a good chance our persecution will come from within the body of Christ itself and institutions we've created in our nation. Pretty soon, our speech may be considered hate speech, and we may find ourselves in prison. Regardless of how it comes and in what form, the only way we will be able to endure is when we have a baptism of holiness. Then, like Jesus and our Egyptian brothers, we will set our face like flint and know that our persecution means we are part of His Kingdom and will be welcomed in with "Well done, My good and faithful servant!"

"Blessed are those who are persecuted for righteousness sake, for the theirs is the kingdom of heaven."

PRACTICAL PRACTICES

CHAPTER 9

Church

Write your findings in a journal or notepad.

Commit to praying for your church. Pray for your pastors and leaders. Pray for boldness, surrender, and holiness to rise up in them and the church as a whole. Pray for an outpouring of the fullness of the Spirit for your church.

Pray for those attending your church to be hungry and thirsty for God.

Pray about your heart (attitude, mindset) towards your church. Ask the Holy Spirit to teach you how to pray for your church.

Home

Are you afraid of persecution?

What do you fear most about persecution? Persecution that comes from other Christians, persecution that comes through words or deeds, or persecution that comes by more violent means?

Is what you're learning making you more determined to share this message with your family or friends? Explain the response you get from them.

Read

Meditate on these verses:

- Read Revelation 1 to 4.
- Read Revelation:1-16.
- Read 2 Peter 1:1-11 and 3:14-18.
- Read 1 Peter 1:3-12 and 3:8-5:19.

Listen

- "Song of Ezekiel" by Paul Wilbur, *Your Great Name*
- "Lord Take Up Your Holy Throne" by Paul Wilbur, *Shalom Jerusalem*
- "There Is One Found Worthy" by Justin Rizzo, Onething Live, *Magnificent Obsession*
- "As in the Days of Noah" by Misty Edwards, *Always on His Mind*

CHAPTER 10

TIME TO STAND

It is hard to write about persecution without referring to Corrie Ten Boom. She and some of her family were put in a concentration camp for hiding and rescuing Jews during WWII. Read this sobering message from a letter she wrote.

The world is deathly ill. It is dying. The Great Physician has already signed the death certificate. Yet there is still a great work for Christians to do. They are to be streams of living water, channels of mercy to those who are still in the world. It is possible for them to do this because they are over-comers.

Christians are ambassadors for Christ. They are representatives from Heaven to this dying world. And because of our presence here, things will change.

My sister, Betsy, and I were in the Nazi concentration camp at Ravensbruck because we committed the crime of loving Jews. Seven hundred of us from Holland, France, Russia, Poland and Belgium were herded into a room built for two hundred. As far as I knew, Betsy and I were the only two representatives of Heaven in that room.

We may have been the Lord's only representatives in that place of hatred, yet because of our presence there, things changed. Jesus said, "In the world you shall have tribulation; but be of good cheer, I have overcome the world." We too, are to be over-comers - bringing the light of Jesus into a world filled with darkness and hate.

Sometimes I get frightened as I read the Bible, and as I look in this world and see all of the tribulation and persecution promised by the Bible coming true. Now I can tell you, though, if you too are afraid, that I have just read the last pages. I can now come to shouting "Hallelujah! Hallelujah!" for I have found where it is written that Jesus said, "He that overcometh shall inherit all things: and I will be His God, and he shall be My son." This is the future and hope of this world. Not that the world will survive - but that we shall be over-comers in the midst of a dying world.

Betsy and I, in the concentration camp, prayed that God would heal Betsy who was so weak and sick. "Yes, the Lord will heal me," Betsy said with confidence. She died the next day and

I could not understand it. They laid her thin body on the concrete floor along with all the other corpses of the women who died that day.

It was hard for me to understand, to believe that God had a purpose for all that. Yet because of Betsy's death, today I am traveling all over the world telling people about Jesus.

There are some among us teaching there will be no tribulation, that the Christians will be able to escape all this. These are the false teachers that Jesus was warning us to expect in the latter days. Most of them have little knowledge of what is already going on across the world. I have been in countries where the saints are already suffering terrible persecution.

In China, the Christians were told, "Don't worry, before the tribulation comes you will be translated - raptured." Then came a terrible persecution. Millions of Christians were tortured to death. Later I heard a Bishop from China say, sadly, "We have failed. We should have made the people strong for persecution rather than telling them Jesus would come first. Tell the people how to be strong in times of persecution, how to stand when the tribulation comes - to stand and not faint."

I feel I have a divine mandate to go and tell the people of this world that it is possible to be strong in the Lord Jesus Christ. We are in training for the tribulation, but more than sixty percent of the body of Christ across the world has already entered into the tribulation. There is no way to escape it. We are next.

Since I have already gone through prison for Jesus' sake, and since I met the Bishop in China, now every time I read a good Bible text I think, "Hey, I can use that in the time of tribulation." Then I write it down and learn it by heart.

When I was in the concentration camp, a camp where only twenty percent of the women came out alive, we tried to cheer each other up by saying, "Nothing could be any worse than today." But we would find the next day was even worse. During this time a Bible verse that I had committed to memory gave me great hope and joy.

"If ye be reproached for the name of Christ, happy are ye; for the spirit of glory and of God resteth upon you; on their part evil is spoken of, but on your part He is glorified." (I Peter 3:14)

I found myself saying, "Hallelujah! Because I am suffering, Jesus is glorified!"

In America, the churches sing, "Let the congregation escape tribulation", but in China and Africa the tribulation has already arrived. This last year alone more than two hundred

thousand Christians were martyred in Africa. Now things like that never get into the newspapers because they cause bad political relations. But I know. I have been there. We need to think about that when we sit down in our nice houses with our nice clothes to eat our steak dinners. Many, many members of the body of Christ are being tortured to death at this very moment, yet we continue right on as though we are all going to escape the tribulation.

Several years ago I was in Africa in a nation where a new government had come into power. The first night I was there some of the Christians were commanded to come to the police station

to register. When they arrived they were arrested and that same night they were executed. The next day the same thing happened with other Christians. The third day it was the same. All the Christians in the district were being systematically murdered.

The fourth day I was to speak in a little church. The people came, but they were filled with fear and tension. All during the service they were looking at each other, their eyes asking, "Will this one I am sitting beside be the next one killed? Will I be the next one?"

The room was hot and stuffy with insects that came through the screenless windows and swirled around the naked bulbs over the bare wooden benches. I told them a story out of my childhood.

"When I was a little girl, " I said, "I went to my father and said, Daddy, I am afraid that I will never be strong enough to be a martyr for Jesus Christ." "Tell me," said Father, "When you take a train trip to Amsterdam, when do I give you the money for the ticket? Three

weeks before?" "No, Daddy, you give me the money for the ticket just before we get on the train."

"That is right," my father said, "and so it is with God's strength. Our Father in Heaven knows when you will need the strength to be a martyr for Jesus Christ. He will supply all you need - just in time."

My African friends were nodding and smiling. Suddenly a spirit of joy descended upon that church and the people began singing,

"In the sweet, by and by, we shall meet on that beautiful shore."

Later that week, half the congregation of that church was executed. I heard later that the other half was killed some months ago. But I must tell you something. I was so happy that the Lord used me to encourage these people, for unlike many of their leaders, I had the word of God. I had been to the Bible and discovered that Jesus said He had not only overcome the world, but to all those who remained faithful to the end, He would give a crown of life.

How can we get ready for the persecution? First we need to feed on the word of God, digest it, make it a part of our being. This will mean disciplined Bible study each day as we not only memorize long passages of scripture, but put the principles to work in our lives.

Next we need to develop a personal relationship with Jesus Christ. Not just the Jesus of yesterday, the Jesus of History, but the life- changing Jesus of today who is still alive and sitting at the right hand of God.

We must be filled with the Holy Spirit. This is no optional command of the Bible, it is absolutely necessary. Those earthly disciples could never have stood up under the persecution of the Jews and Romans had they not waited for Pentecost. Each of us needs our own personal Pentecost, the baptism of the Holy Spirit. We will never be able to stand in the tribulation without it.

In the coming persecution we must be ready to help each other and encourage each other. But we must not wait until the tribulation comes before starting. The fruit of the Spirit should be the dominant force of every Christian's life.

Many are fearful of the coming tribulation, they want to run. I, too, am a little bit afraid when I think that after all my eighty years, including the horrible Nazi concentration camp, that I might have to go through the tribulation also. But then I read the Bible and I am glad.

When I am weak, then I shall be strong, the Bible says. Betsy and I were prisoners for the Lord, we were so weak, but we got power because the Holy Spirit was on us. That mighty inner strengthening of the Holy Spirit helped us through. No, you will not be strong in yourself when the tribulation comes. Rather, you will be strong in the power of Him who will not forsake you. For seventy-six years I have known the Lord Jesus and not once has He ever left me, or let me down.

"Though He slay me, yet will I trust Him", for I know that to all who overcome, He shall give the crown of life. Hallelujah!

Time to Stand

You can't read a story like this without pondering the sobering reality of what awaits us in the form of persecution. It's like a Christian's right-of-passage into God's Kingdom. That is why we must follow the protocol of heaven when walking on the narrow path. No one will be able to endure tribulation—let alone rejoice in it—until we learn to live a life of surrender and holiness.

Our Lord warned us that the effect of following Him will create division, even in our very own households (Luke 21:16). Fathers and sons, mothers and daughters will be foes! Though persecution can take many forms, this kind will most likely be the most profound test of our faith. Persecution may be violent, such as being shot or murdered, or it may mean being arrested and thrown into prison or a concentration camp—yes, within the United Sates! It may mean losing your position even within a Christian organization, or it may manifest through mocking, scorning, slander, gossip, or laughter as you enter a room. Whatever form it takes, we should be able to say, *"The Lord is my helper; I will not fear. What can man do to me?"* (Hebrews 13:6). We don't have to worry—we're eternal!

According to church tradition, not Scripture, the following died "for righteousness sake" by various means:

- Isaiah the prophet died at the order of King Manasseh by being sawn in two with a wood saw.
- Jeremiah was stoned to death by Jews in Egypt.
- Zechariah the prophet was killed by Joash the king between the steps and the altar and then had his blood sprinkled upon the horns of the alter.
- Peter died crucified upside down.
- Andrew died on a X-shaped cross in Greece.
- Matthew was staked or impaled by spears then beheaded.
- Bartholomew, also known as Nathaniel, died in Armenia being flayed to death by a whip.
- James was thrown from a lofty pinnacle of the Temple and then clubbed to death.
- Philip was impaled by iron hooks in his ankles and hung upside down to die.
- James (not Jesus' brother) is believed to have been beheaded by King Herod.
- Jude was crucified in Persia.

- Matthias was apparently stoned then beheaded.
- Paul was tortured then beheaded by the evil Emperor Nero.
- John was exiled on the island of Patmos and died a natural death, but only after being thrown into a pot of boiling oil and miraculously coming out alive.

Other Christians were led into the arenas for sport so that thousands of spectators could watch them be torn asunder by wild beasts. Some suffered torture, forced conversion, and exile, but no matter how bad it was for them or could become for us, His promise has always been, *"I will never leave you nor forsake you"* (Hebrews 13:5b).

A Closing Word

As I said in chapter one, I have spent the last number of years in a prayer of anguish for the body of Christ to wake up and recognize the signs of the times that are upon us and that we will embrace the Holy Spirit because Corrie Ten Boom was right—we are going to need Him. As a result of this anguish, I have suffered mild Christian persecution that came in the form of mocking, avoidance, gossip, and exclusion. But, I've also had the joy of seeing believers wake up and realize that they're famished! God is setting them ablaze and releasing them out into the world. I'll never apologize for waiting on and watching for the Lord's return. He is training me up to have eyes to see and ears to hear. He wants that for all of us.

I find myself sitting on my back deck at night looking at the moon and the stars, telling Him, "I'm listening." I watch the heavens when they speak through eclipses, blood moons, constellations, asteroids, comets, and solar flares, like no other time in history. I watch creation groan as earthquakes and volcanos come to life and hurricanes and storms roar in fierce intensity, like no other time in history. I watch the nations rage and alliances form, moving toward global government, like no other time in history. I watch the days of Lot and days of Noah emerge through increased violence, identity confusion, lust and perversion, like no other time in history. I watch Israel as God gathers the Jews back to the land, as He promised, like no other time in history. And I watch His holy city, Jerusalem, become the burdensome stone as nation after nation try to wipe it off the face of the earth. If you really want to be on God's clock, keep a keen eye on what is happening in Jerusalem.

I close with some of the same questions I started with. Why aren't we being prepared? Why aren't we being taught? Why are the pulpits silent on these matters of Scripture? Why are many in the church not watching? What is going to happen to America when this rich, Laodicean nation we find ourselves in crumbles? How will we respond when we have to lay the bodies of people we know and love side by side during a time of persecution?

Oh, my friends, this study was written out of a place of pure love for you. I pray it has blessed you, even in some small way. I pray it has taken you on your first steps to holiness with Jesus Christ and that you will continue to become a force to be reckoned with upon the earth. I will be praying for you. I look forward to a day when we are all together in heaven with every tear wiped from our eyes. Until then, we have work to do. We must be salt, light, and a city on hill.

I thank you for having the courage to come on this journey through *The Narrow Gate* along the narrow path. We have only just begun, so I encourage you to continue examining yourself and seeking Him with a pure heart. Set aside time to worship Him, to glory in His name, to listen for His voice. Don't be afraid to ask questions in your church. Be bold, be merciful, be pure, be peaceable, be the light. You may feel alone, but we are all on this path with you. May God richly bless you, keep you, and make His face shine upon you and be gracious to you.

May the Lord lift up His countenance upon you and give you…peace (Numbers 6:24-26).

Stay the course. Do not give up. Know that you are not alone. Bless you, my friend!

Carole and the team at Jeremiahs Call: Callie, Heather, Kristine, and Lori

Works Cited

Barna Group. "Jason Malec on Changing Perceptions of the Bible." Video, April 25, 2017, 7:02 minutes. https://www.barna.com/research/jason-malec-changing-perceptions-bible/

Chan, Francis. "Are you Ready for the End?" 2018, 59.33 minutes. https://www.youtube.com/results?search_query=francis+chan+are+you+ready+for+the+end+

Daniel, Keith. "Sermon on the Mount." Video, 2009, 69 minutes. https://www.youtube.com/results?search_query=francis+chan+are+you+ready+for+the+end+

Grace Bible Church. "Boiler Room Prayer." http://www.jerseygrace.org/prayerministry/boiler-room-prayer

Larkin, Clarence. *The Book of Revelation.* Philadelphia, PA, 1919.

Lloyd-Jones, Dr. Martin. "Dying to Self and Beatitudes." Video, April 29, 2016, 48.49 minutes.

https://www.youtube.com/results?search_query=francis+chan+are+you+ready+for+the+end+

Lloyd-Jones, Dr. Martin. *Studies in the Sermon on the Mount*. Grand Rapids, MI: Wm. B. Eerdmans Publishing Co., 1959-60.

Ravenhill, Leonard. *Revival Praying.* Bloomington, MN: Bethany House Publishers, 1962.

Ravenhill, Leonard. *Sodom Had No Bible.* Minneapolis, MN: Bethany House Publishers, 1971.

Spurgeon, Charles. "The Beatitudes" sermon series. Originally delivered 12/21/1873. https://www.youtube.com/results?search_query=charles+spurgeon+beatitudes

Ten Boom, Corrie. Letter from The Hiding Place Message Board. 1974. http://www.libertytothecaptives.net/ten_boom.html

APPENDIX A

TEACHING VIDEOS

To watch the teaching videos to this book visit www.jeremiahscall.org.

Video 1 Baptism of Anguish
https://vimeo.com/279380180

Video 2 Poor in Spirit
https://vimeo.com/279385193

Video 3 Blessed are Those Who Mourn
https://vimeo.com/279397134

Video 4 Blessed are the Meek
https://vimeo.com/279408880

Video 5 Blessed are Those Who Hunger and Thirst for Righteousness
https://vimeo.com/281003792

Video 6 Blessed are the Merciful
https://vimeo.com/279776750

Video 7 Blessed are the Pure in Heart
https://vimeo.com/279794627

Video 8 Blessed are the Peace Makers
https://vimeo.com/280033505

Video 9 Blessed are Those Who Are Persecuted for Righteousness
https://vimeo.com/280039284

Video 10 Time to Stand
https://vimeo.com/280043971

JEREMIAHS CALL

AT JEREMIAHS CALL Ministries, our mission is PREACH. WARN. TEACH. "In Him we preach, warning every man and teaching every man in all wisdom, that we may present every man perfect in Christ Jesus." (Colossians 1:28) We help believers in Christ mature in their faith by unapologetically teaching scriptural truths that challenge us to walk as the ambassadors we are called to be.

Jeremiah was a prophet sent by God to the nation of Israel to sound an awakening alarm to the people during a time when the people compromised the truth of God and were walking in rebellion. He was urging the people to have a change of heart, for truth to be restored, and for people to turn wholly and completely back to the one true God. He was instructed to *"root out and pull down, to destroy and throw down, to build and to plant"* (Jeremiah 1:10).

Jeremiahs Call Ministries (JCM) is exactly that, a call to the heart of each person to wake up, rise up, and walk steadfastly with God! Sharing God's Word in each study will root out, pull down, destroy, and throw down our old selves and then build and plant His nature in our new selves. Shofars, or trumpets, were blown for various reasons in the Bible. One of those reasons was an alarm, an awakening blast calling people to attention to hear a message. God has challenged us to be this kind of ministry.

JCM is a trumpet sound to each and every person, calling you to stand, watch, and walk in the power and authority God gave you as we look to the days ahead. We do this through our transformational Bible studies that are designed to help you grow in your power and authority as a believer of Jesus Christ. Never was there a need for trumpeters to position themselves on the walls of our homes, communities, cities, states, and nation to blast awake sleeping believers than at this very moment. We are committed to preparing the body of Christ for the days ahead.

For more information visit http://www.jeremiahscall.org.

ABOUT THE AUTHOR

Carole L. Urbas, is an ordained Christian minister and has been involved in Christian ministry for nearly twenty years. Having worked for nationally recognized leaders and volunteered with nationally recognized organizations, she took her experience and training to help launch other ministries. After years of in-depth study of God's Word, historical studies, and accounts, as well as participating in Bible studies for over twenty years, she was repeatedly asked to teach and so began writing and teaching studies for both men and women. These projects were brought forth after recognizing a hunger in the body of Christ to learn more about topics—such as Israel, the Middle East, the Holy Spirit, Holiness, the Feasts of the Lord, and Spiritual Warfare—not taught in most churches or Bible study groups.

Carole and her husband, Len, along with their four children reside in Colorado.

For conference inquiries, contact www.jeremiahscall.org

Small Group Leader Questions

Chapter 1

1. Take a little time to get to know one another. Besides learning about family, ask them if they were either raised with a church background or in any other religious faith, and then where they are today.
2. Have each person try to answer the two questions presented in today's teaching:

How would you describe God? Try to look for words that indicate if He's personal to them. If so, in what way is He personal? If God seems distant and "big," try to probe and find out what they believe He is that way.

What does being holy mean to you?

3. If there is still time left, ask the group where they feel the "church" is being trampled underfoot by men, according to the Scripture given in the teaching.

Share prayer requests and close in prayer.

Chapter 2

1. Do you ever feel like there's more to God than what you are currently experiencing? Explain.
2. What is your real estimation of yourself?
3. If we allow God to increase in our lives, what in you must decrease? Explain.
4. Many of us have been doing Christianity a certain way most of our lives, whether we attend a certain type of church or whether we've adopted a particular pattern of thinking. Which mindset do you carry today that is most difficult to change in light of what we're learning about holiness?

Update each other on past prayer requests, share new prayer requests, and close in prayer.

Chapter 3

1. When was the last time you experienced godly sorrow over sin?
2. Do you understand the importance of confession and repentance, not just when you placed your faith in Jesus Christ, but on a regular basis? Do you experience godly sorrow during these times of confession and repentance? In other words, do you see that no matter how small the sin, it still grieves God, meaning it should grieve us too?
3. Have you ever let God grieve through your heart? If so, what was your experience like, whether from your own sin or when He's grieving the sins of the world?
4. Is it difficult for you to move away from old sin patterns? Explain.

5. Many of us do not practice examining ourselves when we enter into a time of prayer. When we practice this and we ask the Holy Spirit to "search our hearts," we open ourselves to a daily cleansing of the Spirit. The Comforter comes in to comfort us with the blessed assurance that we are being transformed from our old nature to our new one. Is this something you are willing to experience each day with God?

Update each other on past prayer requests, share new prayer requests, and close in prayer.

Chapter 4

1. Explain what you know about the Holy Spirit. Based on what you know, does it cause you to be apprehensive towards Him or to embrace Him?
2. Have you yielded to the fullness of the Holy Spirit in your life, meaning do you let the Holy Spirit have full control? If not, what's holding you back? If so, how has it changed your relationship with Christ?
3. Are you hindered in church in how you pray or worship because of what others might think?
4. Are you fearful of the book of Revelation? What comes to mind when you think about that book? Is it new to learn that you are "blessed" when you read it? Will that encourage you to "try" reading it?

Update each other on past prayer requests, share new prayer requests, and close in prayer.

Chapter 5

1. How long have you been a Christian?
2. Where are you striving in your Christian walk?

3. What do you think Scripture means when it says to seek God with all of your heart? To seek Him with all of your strength? To seek Him with all of your soul? And to seek Him with all of your mind?
4. What does Jesus mean when He says to seek His kingdom?
5. If Jesus says that "My kingdom is within you," then how does that change your previous answer?
6. What kind of things are you seeking in your life with all of your strength? With all of your heart? With all of your mind? With all of your soul? (Think in terms of relationships, social life, exercise, travel, family, faith, work, etc.) Compare the time spent in those things with time spent with hungering after righteousness. Give an honest assessment of time spent in each.

Update each other on past prayer requests, share new prayer requests, and close in prayer.

Chapter 6

1. Sit quietly for two minutes as a group and ask God to bring to your spirit any "cries" He wants you to hear right now. Try not to think about what you assume would be a cry but wait patiently for Him to give you a picture, a "knowing," an impression or maybe someone's name. It can be something global, local, or personal.
2. Discuss with the group what you discovered.
3. Besides holidays, how often do you actively show or "act on" showing mercy to others? How much of that is generated by the habit of "doing"? Or, how much is generated—like Jesus when He saw the multitudes—by raw compassion that stirred you to act?

4. Is prayer top priority in your church? Are corporate prayer gatherings common, not once a month, but daily/weekly? Would you consider meeting with the leadership to figure out why it's not a priority and then *how to* make it a priority?

Update each other on past prayer requests, share new prayer requests, and close in prayer.

Chapter 7

1. Understanding that worship is intimately tied into holiness, think about how you worship God. What does your worship look like daily or when you go to church?
2. How active are you in your sanctification process? Is being active in your sanctification a new revelation for you?
3. In what areas does Satan bait you?
4. How have you been taught to view God's laws/commandments? Did the teaching today add any new revelation?

Update each other on past prayer requests, share new prayer requests, and close in prayer.

Chapter 8

1. Is there something in your life that is causing you to fear? (It can be a personal situation, professional, national or global.) Why do you fear this?
2. How do you react to chaos and situations you cannot control? Do you tend to isolate, engage, or something different? Explain.
3. Have you ever been taught about your governmental authority on the earth as an ambassador for Christ? Describe what you've been taught.

4. Where are places and situations you can immediately bring peace to?

Update each other on past prayer requests, share new prayer requests, and close in prayer.

Chapter 9

1. Where has the enemy "stolen, killed, and destroyed" in your life?
2. After listening to the exchange between Peter and Jesus, what kind of stirrings are in your heart about following Him where you may not want to go?
3. Based on what we learned about where and how revivals started, do you believe God could lay His hand on someone like you and use you to restore a sleepy church and usher in revival?
4. What is it costing you now to follow Christ?
5. Does Jesus' promise of a great reward in heaven ease your fears of tribulation or persecution, knowing we are to rejoice when these things occur?

Update each other on past prayer requests, share new prayer requests, and close in prayer.

Chapter 10

1. In what areas do you see your faith maturing?
2. With all of the divisions within the body of Christ today (denominations, beliefs, etc.), what do you think it's going to take for us to become "one"?

3. Are you yielding to the "ministry of the Spirit"? Has this study helped you either *begin or continue* a journey of becoming a walking epistle? Describe.
4. Describe how your prayer life has changed from completing this study?
5. How will you live differently from taking this study *The Narrow Gate*?

Update each other on past prayer requests, share new prayer requests, and close in prayer.

THANK YOU

Thank you for reading *The Narrow Gate*. This is our first book for all generations, bringing encouragement and awakening the Bride of Christ.

Please visit our website: www.Jeremiahscall.org for updates, events, support, and encouragement. Bring your questions, testimonies, and prayers as together we share key insights in the Word of God, personal testimonies, and pray together. Invite a friend and join us!

If interested, contact us at Jeremiahs Call. Explore our social media links and receive additional devotional tips and resources.

CONNECT WITH US

Website: https://www.jeremiahscall.org

Twitter: https://twitter.com/JeremiahsCall5

Facebook: https://www.facebook.com/JeremiahsCallMinistries

Blog: https://www.jeremiahscall.org/blog

Instagram: https://www.instagram.com/jeremiahscallministries

LinkedIn: https://www.linkedin.com/in/jeremiahs-call-ministries-162053161

Teaching Videos: https://www.jeremiahscall.org/videos

Printed by BoD™in Norderstedt, Germany